THE
INSOLENT
CHARIOTS

The Insolent Chariots

BY JOHN KEATS

ILLUSTRATED BY ROBERT OSBORN

J. B. LIPPINCOTT COMPANY

PHILADELPHIA AND NEW YORK

TEXT COPYRIGHT © 1958 BY JOHN KEATS

ILLUSTRATIONS COPYRIGHT © 1958 BY ROBERT OSBORN

PRINTED IN THE UNITED STATES OF AMERICA

LIBRARY OF CONGRESS CATALOG CARD NUMBER 58-12273

THIRD IMPRESSION

The title of this book was suggested by a speech by Mr. Lewis Mumford to the Thirteenth International Congress of Local Authorities, at The Hague, on 12 June, 1957.

This book is thoughtfully dedicated to
the Automobile Manufacturers Association

The chariots shall rage in the streets,
They shall justle one against another in the broad ways:
They shall seem like torches,
They shall run like the lightnings. . . .
                    —NAHUM THE ELKOSHITE, ca. 620 B.C.

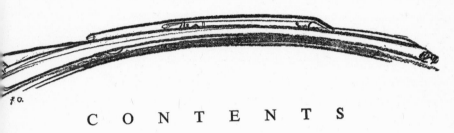

C O N T E N T S

1

THE YEARS OF OUR FORD

ONCE UPON A TIME, the American met the automobile and fell in love. Unfortunately, this led him into matrimony, and so he did not live happily ever after. Cooler heads could have told him the affair was doomed from the start, for in the beginning, the American was poorly prepared to make judgments in such matters. He was merely a rustic Merry Andrew with a cowlick and an adolescent tightening in the groin. In his libidinous innocence, he saw the automobile only as curious, exciting—and obviously willing. Wherefore, he joyfully leaped upon her, and she responded to his caresses by bolting about the landscape in what can only be called a succession of bumps and grinds.

This Arcadian idyll did not persist, of course. Had he loved her and left her, all would have been well. Had he restrained himself, and viewed her as a possible hired woman to be trained for work about the farm and otherwise left strictly alone, all would have been better. But he was innocent; she handed him a likely story and led him to the preacher. Then, before they were fairly out of the churchyard, she began to demonstrate less enchanting aspects of her character. The American, it seems, was trapped by a schemer.

Quickly the automobile became the nagging wife, demanding rubbings and shinings and gifts. She put eyebrows over her windshield in the 1920s, plucked them out in the late 1930s, put them on again in the middle 1940s, and took them off once more in the 1950s. She nagged him for bits of chrome and cursed him for his extravagance when he brought them home. She lifted her face—expensively—from year to year; incessantly demanded new gauds and different colors, developed ever more costly eating habits, threatened to break the family budget and often succeeded, and the American, —poor dolt, not only catered to her whims but decked her out in door-edge guards and silvery Kleenex dispensers.

Since woman from the dawn of time has regarded man as she regards an old house—that is, as something to make over —it is not surprising to note that the automobile wrought dramatic changes in her spouse. Nevertheless, the speed and thoroughness of the transformation is a little awe-inspiring, bespeaking either a weakness on the American's part or a fantastic singleness of purpose on the part of the automobile, or both. For example, in fifty-eight short years the automobile not only became our nation's greatest single topic of conversation, but also unquestionably central to our economy. The automobile became demonstrably more important to us than our human wives, children, jobs and even our food—and I intend to demonstrate this in proper place with fact and figure. The automobile changed our dress, manners, social customs, vacation habits, the shape of our cities, consumer purchasing patterns, common tastes and positions in intercourse.

As the frightful marriage wore on, the automobile's original appeal shrank in inverse proportion to the growth of her demands. She grew sow-fat while demanding bigger, wider, smoother roads. The bigger and better the road, the fatter she became, and the fatter she grew, the greater her demands for even bigger roads. Then, with all the sublety of a madam affecting a lorgnette, she put tail fins on her overblown bustle and sprouted wavering antennae from each fin. And, of course, her every whim was more costly than the last.

In view of these metamorphoses, it is understandable that the American began to stray. In the mid-1950s, he eyed the European car, and found her good. She was petite, she was new, she was gay, she was inexpensive, she bumped and she ground, and like all mistresses, she promised prestige. Maintaining a mistress when one is married to a Harpy is, however, an intolerable situation, and so we can say that the American's marriage to the American automobile is now at an end, and it is only a matter of minutes to the final pistol shot, although who pulls the trigger has yet to be determined.

While it must be borne in mind that the story of our nation's relationship with the American automobile is essentially the story of a love affair, it may serve our purpose equally well to put matters in less emotional terms. For instance, we can look at the thing historically, scientifically, philosophically

13

or geographically, but no matter how objectively we view it, a quality of slapsick tragedy is always apparent.

For example, let's take the historical view. Since 1900 American automobiles have grown longer, lower, wider, faster, jazzier, more complicated and more, much more expensive— but far less efficient and no safer.

Meanwhile, as all the world knows, General Motors is spending millions on automotive research, and this fact has inspired the press to pose scientific questions, For instance, *The New York Times* asked Mr. Edward T. Ragsdale, GM's general manager of the Buick Division, what Buick was doing in 1958 toward achieving fuel economy. "Oh," Mr. Ragsdale said lightly, "we're helping the gas companies, the same as our competitors."

Similarly, we can find nourishment for the mind in the philosophical realm. It is now possible for you to walk across Manhattan Island at rush hour in far less time than you could possibly drive. Twenty years ago, this claim could not have been made. A philosophical question therefore becomes: Will the automobile put man back on his feet?

Equally provocative is the geographical view. In 1900, there was hardly enough paved surface in North America to fill a tooth; today there exists enough to cover New England. In other words, 40,000 square miles of our New World is now under pavement. Our new roads, with their ancilliaries, the motels, filling stations and restaurants advertising Eats, have made it possible for you to drive from Brooklyn to Los Angeles without a change of diet, scenery or culture, and this, too, is a gift of Detroit. Thus, if we assume human progress to be the

14

steady reduction of life's mad chaos into a semblence of order, it is undeniable that the automobile has helped to make such progress by reducing to an easily recognized standard brand that which had once been a frightful confusion of differing peoples, landscapes, and geographical products. Moreover, in our newest cars, it is possible to make the entire trip at a uniform temperature, and so we note that order has been established in the chaos that was once our national climate.

Assuming that America's marriage to its automobile will somehow endure—that the pistol shot will be indefinitely delayed—we can make an objective synthesis of the historical, scientific, philosophical and geographical viewpoints and arrive at accurate predictions. For instance, assuming the marriage to continue in the same course it has followed these last fifty-eight years, simple arithmetic can easily determine the precise moment in time when the last square inch of our continent becomes paved; at what pregnant moment everything is one huge, smooth surface from Hudson's Bay to the Gulf of Mexico.

Then, perhaps, on this vast ballroom floor, everyone will scurry around in a kind of Brownian movement, each couple in its own huge car, going 500 miles an hour, here and there, round and round, up and down, day and night, everyone drinking Coca-Cola and watching color television and listening to the national news broadcast while necking; radar doing the driving and guarding against collision. From time to time the cars will, perhaps, come fleetingly to rest, or—may be—tremble like hummingbirds beside floodlit tinsel filling stations built beside swimming-pooled motels, where car-hopping drum majorettes dressed in boots and tassels dance among the bright bodies of the cars, selling souvenirs and serving electronically-cooked, pre-digested frozen TV suppers on dispensable trays. In all this, only the drum majorettes will not be real. They will be clever illusions wrought by cunning lights to disguise the fact the suppers arrive on conveyor belts out of mechanical kitchens. At any rate, these phantom maidens will summon up Detroit's image of love and beauty, for painful research conducted behind the scenes at national automobile conventions reveals that when an automobile manufacturer dreams of Hebe, he envisions a nubile adolescent who chews gum.

The proof of this Nesselrode will be in the eating, of course, so let us prepare to dine. Let us examine, from the disinterested aspect of eternity, some facts of our life, past and present, and start asking questions.

What, let us wonder, would America have become if the American had not married the automobile? Since such a marriage has taken place, what is the real effect of the automobile on our landscape and on the nature of our society? What are Detroit's real reasons for building what it builds? Why do we really buy the machines we buy? What contribution has Detroit really made to our business community? Is the automobile as essential to us as we might suspect? Just where, pray tell, is Man in the automotive age?

Fortunately for our purposes, Man is pretty easy to find. Here comes one now. We see him in the family shape of Edgar Striver, his wife Sue Ella, and their children Donna and Ralph. Together with their dog, Fred, they are part of a slowly

moving line of traffic inching through New England on the hottest July day in fifty years. They have started and stopped eighty-seven times in the last three hundred yards on Rhode Island's Route 30. It is late afternoon, they're trying to get to Providence, but there's an accident up ahead and the Strivers are still two miles south of Nooseneck. Fred is carsick. Donna and Ralph are fighting and dripping fried clams onto the new seat covers. Edgar and the radiator are approaching the boiling point, Sue Ella's hair is uncoiling on the nape of her neck and her face is livid with fatigue and the radio is blaring away. The announcer is telling them that for that extra go, for that power the jet jockeys know, for the gasoline that keeps your motor clean, see your Powerblast dealer today. Here is a typical family group in these years of our Ford. Here are four free American pilgrims off to visit Plymouth Rock to have their faith in our institutions renewed. They are on vacation, driving their car, masters of their fates, captains of their souls. They are the idealized family version of Prometheus Unbound.

Man in the automotive age? He is everywhere. Here comes another, Richard Masters by name, encapsulated in chromium, ruler of three hundred and fifty horses which are now drawing him at sixteen miles an hour through downtown Washington, D.C.—for sixteen miles an hour is Washington's top average downtown speed, our traffic scientists say. Masters has entered the world of no U turn, no left turn, no right turn, right turn only, stop, go, one way, slow, no parking from 8:30 A.M. to 6 P.M. and no standing. He is looking for a place to park, along with 350,000 other people.

Man is everywhere in this age, and often his wildest dreams are fulfilled, just as even the worst of marriges boasts random moments of ecstacy. Here is one other we might consider—Howard Blatant. Howard is whizzing down the Pennsylvania Turnpike's northeast extension at 82.7 miles an hour true ground speed. He rests on cushions, rides on air, soothed by music. He is completely and deeply content as he hurtles along in a two-ton Thunderbolt with a momentum of 487,200 pounds per foot per second. Protected from wind, sound and jolt, Howard idly watches the scenery glide past. It seems to move slowly, for the road is straight, wide and apparently endless. Howard stares ahead, lost in an ineffable trance, but he will not fall asleep . . . will not fall asleep . . . will not fall asl . . . will not fall . . . will not fa . . . will not . . . Mr. Blatant has two seconds left.

Man in the automotive age? He is everywhere; it is an easy question to answer. It may be a little more difficult to answer why he is there, and if he knows where he is, but let's take a cut at it. It should be a lot of good, clean fun.

"WHENCE AND WHAT ART THOU, EXECRABLE SHAPE?"

—Paradise Lost

YEAR BY YEAR the American population is growing taller, and year by year American automobiles are growing lower. Dispassionate research indicates that the average roof of today's American car rises no higher than the average belly-button in Oklahoma. In any case, gone are the days when one could step into one's car, sit up straight in the driver's seat, wearing a hat, and command a view of the front fenders, the curb and the white line. Now, one crouches to crawl into an illuminated rolling cave, and then reclines on a sort of couch, there to push buttons and idly wonder what might lie in front of the glittering hood, while the sun burns into the eyes through the slanted windshield that is strangely overhead.

On most American pavement, a speed of more than 50 miles an hour is illegal, yet American speedometers indicate the possibility of hitting 140. At the same time, some manufacturers supply a buzzer that sounds when one reaches 50, in order to induce a feeling of guilt.

In times past, a dented fender cost perhaps eight dollars to repair. Today, mechanics must strip the entire side from the machine to iron out an insignificant wrinkle, and the cost of this operation often exceeds that of a Caesarean section.

While automobiles grow ever lower, faster and more costly to buy and repair, our cities become more and more congested—the average speed falls well below the theoretical maximum city speed limits—and it has been estimated that if one foot were chopped off the lengths of all its automobiles, New York City would gain 80 additional miles of usable streets.

Little contradictions of this sort suggest that American automobile design is steadily proceeding away from reality with the speed of light, and we might profitably wonder if this is true, and if so, why? Perhaps we might first wonder why our automobiles are so much alike that Detroit designers no longer worry about the general shape of their competitors' cars, but simply about the number of square inches of chromium they might carry next year. Great truths often have rude sources, so let us begin with one mechanic's explanation:

"Leave a Ford and a Chevy overnight in the same garage," he said, "and nine months later you get a Plymouth."

This dictum is essentially correct. Nine months is a normal gestative period, and automobiles do enjoy a singular penchant for cross-breeding. Further investigation, however, discloses that wherever cross-breeding occurs among automobiles, the result is always a more expensive combination of the least desirable features of the parents. A curious example is the apparent child of the Ford Thunderbird and the Reo Wolverine.

The pureblood Thunderbird resembles a sports car, which is to say, a car so small, low, uncomfortable, swift and exposed to the elements that driving it is apt to be a sporting proposition, in much the same sense that Russian roulette can be considered a sporting proposition. The sports car is specifically designed for the perpetual adolescent who feels a need to play at being a latter-day Barney Oldfield in an Ivy League beanie. Its tremendous agility is an open invitation to break the owner's head, or the law, or both, and therefore we can say that the adolescent who buys it is delinquent, and so, for that matter, is the manufacturer who sells it. At any rate, the Thunderbird mated with the Wolverine which thirty years ago, was considered a practical family car.

Low powered, soundly built, the Wolverine had convenient running boards and a weatherproof cab in which two parents could ride in blessed isolation from their teeming get, who huddled in an open rumbleseat behind them. Since parents like to be alone, warm and dry, and since children like to be uncomfortable and by themselves, the Wolverine adequately met every family's need. The only problem the Wolverine presented was that the rumbleseat was singularly easy to climb out of while the car was bounding along at 40 miles an hour.

The Thunderine, as we might as well call it, is a mutant. In its convertible aspect, gone are the handy runningboards; gone is the weatherproof cab. No trace of the Reo's low power remains. The Thunderine is simply a more costly, longer Thunderbird with a rumbleseat, and the family that rides in it enjoys a feeling of togetherness. In a Thunderine, everyone is as unsafe and as uncomfortable as the children, and as delinquent as the owner.

Another illustration of our general rule is the mutant we know as the "hardtop convertible." This is a car whose top is neither hard nor convertible.* You cannot put the top up; you cannot put it down. It will not protect you in case of accident. Turn a hardtop's wheels up on the pavement, and the top will collapse like a Japanese lantern, for it has no center posts to support it. Even an upside-down convertible-convertible will rest on its centerposts.

While the convertible-convertible is breezy and the sedan is stuffy, the hardtop is simply draughty when it is not too hot or too cold. In summer days you must keep the windows open lest the sun, beating through the hardtop's expanse of glass, cook you like a cruller. In winter days the windows serve only to illustrate the proposition that the insulated sedan is, after all, warmer. Conforming to the general rule for automotive mutants, the hardtop is more expensive than either parent. Normally, you would not conceive of a reasonable man buying such a curious anomaly, and sober investigation discloses that such a man does not *choose* to do so; that the contraption is no more designed for him than is the sports car.

Supposing a reasonable man were to try to buy an American automobile, however, what choice remains? Surely he will not buy a dreamboat, which is to say, a Chinese love junk, or perpetual Wurlitzer—that vast, neon-lit pinball machine with the chromium schmaltz, the pushbuttons, the

---

* There is also a sub-mutant—a hardtop that *does* convert with aid of a fantastic amount of expensive machinery modeled after the mounting of the disappearing coastal guns of 1864.

multiple batteries of headlamps and the glitter of tail fins that Detroit calls the luxury automobile. Reasonable men, who generally have more brains than money, are content to leave the purchase of dreamboats up to crooners, Texans, gamblers and athletes.

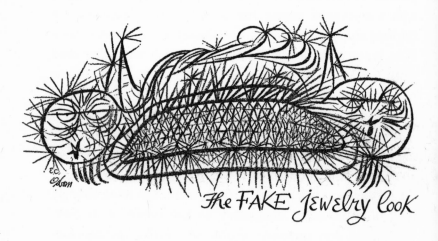

The FAKE Jewelry look

Unfortunately, there is nothing on the American automobile market that is not either a sports car or a dreamboat, or some mutant that resembles the one more than it resembles the other. Further, all share generic characteristics that have little to do with outward shape. All American automobiles cost too much. All fall apart within roughly the same time limits. With every passing year, the spark plugs become increasingly difficult to get at. Thus, no real choice presents itself to the reasonable man, and this is a pity because the entire nation might reasonably be expected to welcome the Second Coming of the Model T.

For the benefit of readers born since the Hoover administration, who know only the baroque period of automobile design, I will say that Henry Ford's Model T represented the end of man's long search for an adequate substitute for the horse—a search that began one day in 1649 when an ingenious Teuton managed to move a wagon for fifteen minutes with a clockwork motor. Just as Rome never regained the spiritual strength she knew at mid-point in the Second Punic War, automobile design has never known a finer hour than when the Model T appeared in 1908, looking as one historian observed, as though it had been drawn by an unusually backward child in the lower grades.

The thing shimmied, jittered, wheezed, clanked and rattled, but it ran. It was light, was only a hundred inches long, could turn in a twelve-foot circle, was high enough to clear the high crowns of rutty farm roads, and it was more strongly built of better metal than many an automobile of its time. The engine was perfectly capable of meeting the demands made on it, could run on a solution of kerosene and old candle ends, and the entire contraption was not only easy to understand but simple to repair. Finally, it was comparatively cheap, but this is not to say that the first Model T was a cheap car. The Model T touring car was put on the Market at $850, a price that—considering the average income of the time—made it relatively more expensive than the 1949 Ford. Still, other automobiles of 1908 cost nearly three times more than the Model T and possessed fewer advantages. Unlike its competitors, the Ford was mass-produced, had standard parts that were everywhere available, and it was backed by a reliable service warranty. Henry Ford made his profit on volume sales and raised wages while driving the price down and down. When the average car was selling for $2,137.56 and the average man earned a dollar a day, Henry Ford was able to hang a $500 price tag on his creation. Later, he drove the price to $365, and the saying grew, "One day, one dollar; one year, one Ford." In sum, the Model T was a simple, practical, tough, economical means of transportation well suited to the American mind of the time, and well suited to the income and to the roads of the period. There was never such a car before or since.

In view of the Model T's widespread acceptance, it seems proper to wonder why the thing is no longer made, or perhaps, it is more proper to wonder why, with our increased technical ability, there is not now a cheap, safe, practical, simple, sturdy and economical American automobile on the road. Consider the station wagon for a moment—a contraption currently advertised as the perfect, practical family car.

Here is a mutant out of a dreamboat by a truck. Conforming to our rule, the station wagon is more expensive than either parent of the same size. Neither sturdy nor safe, it combines the truck's rattles with the dreamboat's speed and crumple-ability. Instead of being blessed with the truck's economical diesel engine, it possesses the dreamboat's high-octane gas-gulper. If you put the same load in the station wagon's bed that you can put in a truck bed the same size, the station wagon settles down on its axles, because it has the dreamboat's springs instead of the truck's. And—as far as being a perfectly designed family vacation car is concerned, look here:

26

Tim and Kim Vandervogel and their three children are spinning along the turnpike, headed for northern forests. The parents share the front seat, the kids sit in the seat behind them, and the back of the station wagon is packed tight with the tent, the bedrolls, the Primus stove and assorted paraphernalia. It took Tim three hours to pack everything just so, but it all went in and no one was inconvenienced. So the Vandervogels are rolling merrily along, singing as the miles slide past, and then the rear tire goes flat.

And where, pray tell, is the spare tire?

No, it's not on the running board—there are no running boards.

No, it's not on the tailgate, and it isn't on the roof with the canoe, nor is Kim holding it in her lap.

Yes, gentle reader, it's under the floorboards, and what do you think is on the floorboards above the spare tire compartment? Why the camping equipment, naturally.

So Tim climbs out, unpacks the camping gear, filches out the spare tire, changes wheels, puts the deflated tire back under the floorboards, and spends the next random hours repacking the camping gear which he will have to unpack and repack again at the next garage.

Tim had hardly resumed his journey the following day when he discovered another curious flaw in his station wagon's design as a practical vacation car: it had no more road clearance than a dreamboat. Thus, Tim left a generous slather of odd bits of broken metal on the rocky crown of an old Adirondack logging road when he ventured off the highway and into the forest of his midsummer's desire. (One tow-truck and $87 later, he went home.)

If Detroit were to build an honest-to-goodness family vacation car for athletes like the Vandervogels—and people who *look* like the Vandervogels are shown simpering at us from every station wagon advertisement—it would seem logical that such a car would not only have high road clearance but more enduring paint, a larger gas tank, stiffer springs, a truck transmission and four-wheel drive. In short, it would be a machine able to go anywhere in any weather and it would resemble an Army weapons carrier, complete to water cans, shovels and picks strapped to its sides.

As matters stand, however, the station wagon can go nowhere and do nothing that is forbidden to the dreamboat. It is as far removed from any station as it is from any wagon. Its front seat is as pillowy as any dreamboat's but its back seats are hard, flat and emit a chorus of ill-assorted squeaks and odd bird-songs. Because of the hump in the middle of its front-seat floor, it can comfortably be used as a dreamboat by only two people—the driver and one passenger. For the back seat riders, it is only half a dream, and the worse half at that. Because the rear space can never be entirely loaded, it is only half a wagon. When Tim lowered the rear seats to form one big, flat deck for his three children, the kids clamored to have him put the seats back up again before he'd gone ten miles. Their tiny rumps had had it, chum, and so the deck disappeared, the seats reappeared, and Tim moodily reflected he might as well have bought a reasonably comfortable two-door sedan. He could have saved himself $2,000.

Therefore, we can say that the station wagon, like every

other contraption Detroit produces, can be a snare and a delusion, but the Automobile Manufacturers Association says it produces only what the public demands.

Does Detroit have the nation by the ear, forcing America to accept whatever it decides to bring forth?

Or, can it be that the public is demanding over-long, over-powered, uneconomical, impractical automobiles, the cheapest of which costs more than a college education?

Oddly enough, the answer to both questions is Yes. To understand why this should be so, we must briefly review our automotive history.

No one designed the automobile—it was merely put together, more or less by chance, in 1895, when a Frenchman installed a German's engine in a wagon by means of a series of typically Gallic compromises with reality. The engine was one of Germany's few failures in an otherwise exemplary technical history. The piston thrice went up and down within the cylinder before an explosion finally moved something worth moving. The Frenchman, one M. Levassor, placed this monstrosity before his cart, apparently on the theory that it would replace the horse.

Since the engine ran on a constant setting, a series of gears and a disengaging clutch had to be devised to make possible smooth transitions in speed. Since the rear wheels were to supply the push (God knows why) the drive shaft had to be carried from the front of the wagon to the rear axle.

I know, it sounds silly, but there it is. And there, I might add, the automobile has remained. Today's dreamboats are basically M. Levassor's 1895 Panhards, differing only in detail. Their engines by and large are still idiotically in front, replacing horses, and they are still the same lugubrious Teutonic devices which spend three revolutions wearing themselves out before belching out a fourth to move you an inch. The drive shaft, the clutch and the gears are with us yet, still as unnecessary a series of mechanical compromises as you are likely to find in a long, tiresome search.

The sound reason for this state of affairs is that not one of the automobile's first builders—neither the Europeans nor their American imitators—was an inventor of the least repute. None had a sound training in mechanical engineering and as Merrill Dennison points out in his book, *The Power to Go,** only two could be called superior mechanics. The bleak fact is that our automotive engineers were merely a gaggle of village pipefitters.

When Henry Ford came late to this pipefitters' convention, the automobile had already captured the public imagination, and Mr. Ford's contribution was to sell dirt cheap. It did not occur to him to invent a new automobile. He simply borrowed then-current ideas. Next, he borrowed the mass production techniques that had already made Ransom E. Olds a millionaire, and in order to cut costs to the nub, he froze the Model T's design for nineteen years and told the customers they could have any color they wished "as long as it was black." Whereupon, Mr. Ford started stamping out Model Ts like a madwoman with a cookie cutter, and 15,000,000 sales later, America was on wheels for keeps.

Until Mr. Ford arrived on the scene, automobile design

---

* Doubleday, New York, 1956.

was a fluid thing, and the fact that it has solidified may be attributed to the pipefitters' lack of imagination. After Mr. Ford, design remained essentially that of the 1895 Panhard because the cars *did* run, and nobody felt like arguing with success. So we can say that Mr. Ford's standardization of parts also froze automobile design for good, and the only subsequent changes have been made in the details. For instance, no one thought of designing a radically new engine— all efforts were concentrated on making the old engine better by some means of improved ignition, better valves, and so on. Ironically enough, every improvement, such as higher compression, merely made the engines more complicated, more

difficult to repair, and more expensive to manufacture and operate. In 1928, for example, motorists were getting about fifteen miles to a gallon of gasoline. Today, they are getting close to that mileage, but the engines have two to four more cylinders, greater power, higher compression, and demand a more expensive gasoline. Thus, even when we take into account the general inflation of prices and wages since 1928, today's motorist spends relatively more to travel the same number of miles and if he obeys the speed laws, he gets there no sooner.*

Mr. Ford's contribution did not end with his standardization of design, however. More significantly, he put the automobile within reach of the merest human utensil. He thus freed the peasant from his Kansas clods, enabled the wage slave to live miles from his useful toil, brought the Bronx to the Catskills, took the front porch off the house in favor of the Sunday drive, substituted the back seat for the village haymow, simplified the problem of the bank robber's getaway, and changed the whole pattern of American life. By 1929, there were nine million more automobiles in America than there were telephones and the automobile industry was already the nation's largest. Today, 10,000,000 Americans are directly or indirectly employed in the manufacture, sale or maintenance of automobiles; one of every six business firms is in some way dependent on the automotive industry; more than one-

---

* Turnpikes, of course, provide motorists with an important exception to this rule. Turnpikes often cut mileage and save time—but not money. In any event, this is a case where the road is doing something for the motorist that the design of the motorist's automobile does not.

third of the nation's intercity travel is by motor bus; more than 6,000 towns without rail or water transportation are absolutely dependent on automobiles, buses and trucks for their very existence. During World War II, the government discovered so many workers used automobile transportation that 24,000,000 cars had to be kept running if we were to supply goodies to the troops, and this figure would be much higher today, what with the tremendous increase in suburban development. There is little reason to prolong a statistical recital—the fact is that American life is now so bound up in so many ways to the automobile that ownership of a car is no longer a rich man's privilege, but a common necessity. In this sense, the answer to the question, Does Detroit force America to accept whatever it decides to bring forth, is Yes. If you need a car—and you probably imagine that you do—you must buy one, and sales statistics say the chances are twenty to one you will buy one from Detroit, and nearly fifty-fifty that you will buy from General Motors.

The answer to our other question, Does the public demand over-long, over-powered, uneconomical, impractical and too-expensive automobiles, is also Yes, but with important qualifications. Once again, we will have to plunge into history to see why this should be so.

Like any primitive people confronted with an inexplicable phenomenon, Americans were quick to assign mystical characteristics to the automobile when it first appeared among them. They sang devotional hymns—"My Merry Oldsmobile" and "Gasoline, Gasoline," are examples that speed to the mind

—and they personified the new deity and assigned its animal qualities as well. These attitudes persist today, for Mr. Bellamy Partridge writes in his *Fill Her Up!* * of the motorist's "real affection for the faithful old bus.

"It was somewhat like the relationship between a boy and his dog," Mr. Partridge explains. "He [the motorist] knew the car was getting old and stiff in the joints, but it was doing the best it could and he loved it. He began to take better care of it. He cleaned and polished it himself. . . . The knocking of the old car as it climbed a hill . . . hurt like sticking a knife between his ribs, and he could draw a long breath of relief as they reached the top. Instead of being glad to see the old bunch of junk go when his new car was ready for delivery, the owner felt a little tug in the neighborhood of his heart. I stood watching a motorist one day when he was turning in his old car . . . and when he thought nobody was looking, he slipped over and patted the battered old veteran on the bonnet as if to say, 'You've been a faithful old wagon, and I hope you'll get a good home.' Then he hurried over to his new car, stepped in, and drove away without another look. I knew just how he felt, for I had felt that way, myself. . . ."

Could this passage be played with violin accompaniment? Certainly. Anthropomorphism? Yes, and personification, too. Incredible? No, on the contrary. Mr. Partridge's bathos is widely shared. In *Bright Wheels Rolling* † a book Mr. Ken Purdy wrote for an automobile-collecting tenor named Mr. James Melton, Mr. Purdy has Mr. Melton say: "These cars

---

* McGraw Hill, New York, 1952.
† Macrae-Smith Company, Philadelphia, 1954.

are living things; they have being, entity, individuality of their own. They have moved about the world, they have witnessed great events."

Similarly, we find sports car enthusiasts assigning magical virtues to their little kidney-breakers. A sports car is "like a good dancing partner," one told *Popular Mechanics* magazine; "a good sports car seems to anticipate the driver's actions . . . together, car and driver are a team, like a polo player and his pony."

In short, automobiles were love-objects from the start, venerated, called friends, lovingly polished and assigned the virtues of ponies, veterans and dogs. When we view matters in this light, it is easy to see why Americans are as apt to lavish gee-gaws on their automobiles as Hindus are to deck their idols out with gold and jewels. It was the singular American propensity to do so that led to the death of the Model T, and to the opening of the period of baroque design.

It is most usually said of Mr. Ford that he was a simple, common man; indeed, it would be difficult to find a man more common, or, in many ways, more of a simpleton. Henry wanted a no-nonsense, good, cheap car to use around the farm, and when he produced the Model T, that, said Hank, was that. Up to this point, Mr. Ford was exactly in touch with the desires of the common man. But Mr. Ford did not understand the truth of Kant's statement that all things excellent are as difficult as they are rare. By producing 15,000,000 Tin Lizzies (to use the anthropomorphological name) Mr. Ford made them just a bit too common, and too much familiarity too soon bred too much contempt. As *Harper's* maga-

35

zine remarked, "as soon as the customers could see that the supply of cars was infinite, they began to want the style and variety that Ford, by temperament and principle, denied them." Even in the early days of the Model T, a hundred businesses were born to supply little fripperies and conveniences that Henry hadn't seen fit to install on the assembly line. By 1927, Chevrolets were whizzing around in brighter colors and with fancier gauds, and Ford was no longer the best-selling car in America. A prudent man himself, Old Henry simply couldn't understand what was happening. Why couldn't people see that his Model T was the only car anywhere that gave the customer anything remotely resembling his money's worth? Style? Doodads? Old Henry certainly couldn't see them. It is tempting to wonder what Old Henry would think of today's flamboyant Fords, and of Mr. George William Walker, the current Ford company's vice president in charge of styling.

While Mr. Ford was spare, frugal and derisive of his laborers, *Time* magazine says Mr. Walker is a friendly fat man who uses perfume, owns seventy suits, kisses the factory hands' babies and labors mightily in a $50,000 private office only slightly smaller than the Taj Mahal—an office tastefully decorated in black and white, boasting a wall full of high-fidelity phonographs, television sets, refrigerators and hidden cabinets.

Where Mr. Ford locked up his design department and hid the key for nineteen years in order to keep costs and prices low, Mr. Walker's design department spends $1,600,000 a year on pencils and other supplies alone.

While Mr. Ford dressed like a Baptist deacon in mourning and uncompromisingly drove somber black automobiles, Mr.

Walker's taste is different. Recalling his "finest moment"—it came during a trip to Miami—Mr. Walker told *Time* magazine:

"I was terrific. There I was in my white Continental, and I was wearing a pure-silk, pure-white, embroidered cowboy shirt, and black gabardine trousers. Beside me in the car was my jet-black Great Dane, imported from Europe, named Dana Von Krupp. You just can't do any better than that."

While Old Henry thought value for the money was what sold a car, Mr. Walker says, "Beauty is what sells the American car. And the person we're designing it for is the American woman. It is the woman who likes colors. We've spent millions to make the floor covering like the carpet in her living room."

Before we doubt that Mr. Walker's theories are entirely correct, it would be well to consult with the Chrysler Corporation's bookkeepers. For many years, Chrysler enjoyed the reputation—among engineers—of building sound engineering into

What a vulgarity!—

its products. This led the corporation to the mistaken assumptions (1) that the reputation was generally understood by the public and (2) that the public bought cars on some kind of rational basis. So, in 1954, thinking to meet the public mood and need—but really matching the desires of its pragmatic engineers—Chrysler produced an un-frilly, shorter, sturdier, easier-to-park automobile and waited for the money to pour in.

Sales dropped by half.

Petulantly, Chrysler went back into the market in 1955 with a car three inches lower, sixteen inches longer, blazing with three colors and boasting higher tail fins than anything this side of a B-29.

Sales soared.

Tide magazine congratulated Chrysler on one of the most remarkable comebacks in financial history, but Detroit shrugged. To Ford and to General Motors, Chrysler's experience was simply additional proof of Phineas T. Barnum's Law of Applied Economics which states: "There's a sucker born every minute."

Considering Chrysler's lesson and the general applicability of Barnum's Law, it is tempting to say, Yes, the public is chiefly responsible for the design of the cars it buys. Witness the Detroit secretary who took one look at this year's new cars and sighed, "Chrome is my favorite color." Then, there is the Pontiac dealer, who says:

"A guy comes in and says all he wants is transportation. He doesn't want a thing on his car—not even a heater. So we take him over to a dog and he looks at the thing, and then he starts to wander around the shop, and it turns out what he really wants is the hardtop with everything on it. Only, he doesn't want to pay for it. The trouble with the public is that what it wants is a ten-cent Cadillac."

Before we jump to our conclusions, however, it is well to know that Detroit's designers are the first to say that the public's taste has nothing in the world to do with the shape of today's cars. For example, Mr. William Mitchell, General Motors' director of styling, told *Fortune* magazine in June, 1956, "We have to do something more than just create something people think is nice.

"To us, that's a dirty word [nice]," Mr. Mitchell explained. "You don't dare lose your guts in this business."

Nor is safety of paramount concern to Detroit's designers. One of Mitchell's assistants told *Fortune's* reporter:

"If we made a car that was completely safe to ride in, I wonder whether it would sell."

Of course it wouldn't, Mr. Mitchell replied. Such a car, he said, would appeal only to "squares—and there ain't any squares no more."

Thus, Mr. Mitchell and kindred designers talk of Detroit's higher task—that of selling cars to unsquares who "do not yet know what they need." It is to General Motors' credit that it discovered, or sensed, that the public's desperate, but unknown, unvoiced need was not for a completely safe automobile, but for tail fins. Mr. Henry J. Earl, a GM vice president of styling, thereupon boldly placed them on the 1948

Cadillac and earned undying fame as Detroit's fin father.

While Mr. Mitchell and the bulk of his psychic confreres thus manfully help to save the public the effort of introspection, a few carpers within the industry wonder if this is really the right course to take.

"Designers are briefed 'to give the public what it wants,' " Mr. Raymond Loewy wrote in *The Atlantic Monthly*, "and 'what the public wants' is being translated into the flashy, the gadgety, the spectacular."

Mr. Loewy, an industrial designer of international reputation, whose partnership and companies bearing his name have provided designs for more than a hundred corporations ranging from cosmetics houses to railroads, has been a Studebaker designer since 1938. In his *Atlantic* article in 1955—which was also a speech he made to the fifth annual meeting of the Society of Automotive Engineers—Mr. Loewy said:

40

"I refuse to believe that today's automobiles represent . . . 'what the public wants' . . . and the result of this mistaken opinion is vulgarity and blatancy. Instead of the automobile's expressing advancement, the story is now one of external bric-a-brac. This reflects a distorted notion of what is competitive.

"Every really creative and imaginative stylist and many engineers I know seem to be frustrated in their work today."

Whether you listen to Mr. Mitchell or to Mr. Loewy, the result seems to be the same—the public is usually not consulted. Moreover, if you are thinking of buying an American automobile next year, you may be absolutely sure that what you think *this* year is of no importance to Detroit, because Detroit is already committed to produce in 1960 an automobile that it designed in 1957. For example, it was the author's privilege to inspect in 1956 the design of the Buick that went on sale in 1958, and as a Buick dealer confided when the 1958 models went on display, "you can see it's the same old dog we were selling in '57.

"Only," he said, "at the last minute, they changed the '58 design to put that two-inch chrome strip on the back fenders to look like a tail fin. That lets me tell the customers it's an all-new car, the best Buick yet, and stuff like that."

In a way, the whole question of whether Detroit or the public makes taste is moot; the only certainty in the affair is that changes are made from year to year, and that the changes are all minor, with the exception of the annual change in price. Thus, there was no sudden leap from Henry Ford's alpaca coat to Mr. Walker's silk cowboy shirt; from Mr.

Ford's black touring car to Mr. Walker's white Continental. Once again, history provides a demonstration:

From the moment the 1895 Panhards appeared, Europeans have provided all the significant thinking, so to speak, in automobile design. The American genius is ever imitative, rather than original, and so our 1903 productions were drawn after the De Dion-Boutons and Renaults of the time. Later, the lines of the ancient Fiat racer were plagiarized by our Stutz Bearcat and Mercer Runabout, and are still to be seen in our Thunderbirds and Corvettes. Likewise, the technical improvements have always come from abroad. For instance, Europeans have been using air suspension for several years. Fluid transmissions first appeared in boats in 1900, and in English buses in 1926. They did not show up in American vehicles until 1938. Direct driveshafts, split axles, torsion bars—these and a hundred other innovations were proved in Europe before they drifted across the Atlantic. Indeed, the only features of current European cars that we have not imitated have been economical, air-cooled engines, located

Hispano-Suiza.
(Ozenfant (1911) Carrosserie

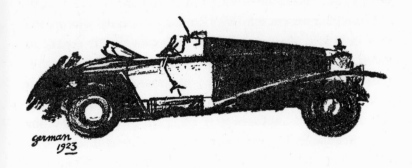

german
1923

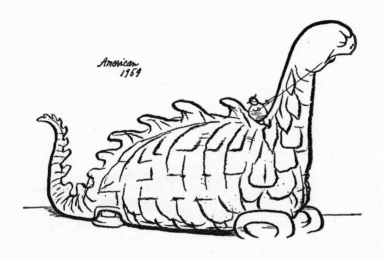

American
1969

in the rear, and functional body designs. There is hope such features will eventually appear in American automobiles, if only because we seem to have copied everything else. American imitations always manage to carry an uniquely American flavor, however, and considering Detroit's performance to date and national predelictions in general, it seems likely that when we finally get around to building a small car, we will build the world's biggest small car, or, perhaps, the world's smallest big car. In any event, it will doubtless be equipped with radar light-dimmers, fatter tires, FM radio; pushbutton windows, seats and aerials; power steering, power brakes, central heating, air conditioning, enough electrical equipment to illuminate Boston, overdrive, fuel injection, and a tinted wrap-around windshield that wets itself. As Mr. M. M. Musselman points out in his *Get a Horse!* * when Detroit imitates, it is as though a hack artist copied the Mona Lisa, adding a Pepsodent smile, red hair, and a rhinestone tiara. †

Apart from the normal time it takes an European idea to swim the ocean, there seem to be three chief reasons why

---

* J. B. Lippincott Company, Philadelphia, 1950.

† The pattern to date seems to be that a small car inevitably grows larger. When the Army peep returned from Hitler's War to become the civilian jeep, it discarded its short wheelbase, its useful four-wheel drive and its combat tires and evolved into a convertible roadster practically impossible to sell. Likewise, when nagged by foreign car sales to the point where it decided to get in on the act, General Motors brought to this country some of the small cars manufactured by its European subsidiaries—but not before making them somewhat larger and adding chromium. Again, the Ford Thunderbird first appeared in pint size, then added a rumbleseat; now appears as a four-door hardtop dreamboat, j.g. Even American Motors allowed its first small car to grow larger, but now, finger on the public pulse, is shrinking them back to size. J.K.

Detroit makes changes so slowly in automobile design and engineering. They are: (1) the rustic caution and provincial limitations of the Midwestern mind, (2) creeping Charlie Wilsonism and (3) the need for maintaining a relatively high used car price.

The first reason is almost self-explanatory. It will be remembered that our automotive pioneers were humble men; they had something of the hayseed's fear of being laughed at. It is doubtful whether Detroit has yet got over the embarrassment of equipping the first automobile bodies with whipsockets. Ah, the Midwest! Land of simple plowmen! No doubt it was the Midwesterners' immemorial custom of attending agricultural fairs which led them all to think in terms of the biggest pumpkins, and thus to believe that if it's the biggest, it's the best, no matter whether this means digging the world's deepest sunken garden, or winning the most football games, or building the world's biggest, gaudiest cars. The essential conservatism of the phrase, "the biggest means the best," is easily seen when we construe it to mean "more of the same." If the automobile had been conceived and built entirely within New England, it might have been small, simple, practical and exquisitely machined. But, alas, it was brought forth in greatest numbers in the expansive, slap-dash world of Babbitt and Elmer Gantry. Now, it has given the Midwest's culture to the nation; Detroit has shaped us in its image. Today, most Americans join in the shout, "The biggest means the best!" and the echo responds from Detroit, "More of the same!"

Moreover, Detroit's insularity is rather overwhelming.

Writing in the *Reporter* magazine last April, Eric Larrabee correctly attributed this to (1) the traditional "solid, middle-brow" qualities of the Midwestern mind and (2) to the kind of padded cell Detroit has contrived for itself. Mr. Larrabee says that Detroit executives, thinking of the fantastic effect their orders for raw materials and labor have on the nation, just sort of naturally conclude that what is good for General Motors must of course be good for America. He also reports what every other observer of Detroit has discovered: Detroit's executives (and their wives) talk to no one but each other, and wherever they talk, be it at home, in conference, at luncheon, or at the Bloomfield Hills country club, the only thing they talk about is automobiles.

Such a one-track conversation has resulted in Detroit's sealing itself off from the rest of the nation, so that news from the outside world takes a considerable time to filter in to the center of town, if it filters in at all. Whenever such news contains criticism, Detroit presents a bitter, united front. For instance, Detroit has recently learned the public is somewhat disenchanted with Detroit's dreamboats. Detroit's reaction was typical, even predictable. First, Detroit assumed the outside world couldn't possibly understand Detroit's problems, much less make suggestions. Therefore, criticism of dreamboats was without merit. Second, Detroit blamed everything on Walter Reuther. Then, catching fire from an old, almost completely dead coal buried deep in the ashes of the Midwestern mind, Detroit decided there really weren't any problems, after all, and that the criticism was nothing but a lot of nittering and nattering emanating from a few aesthetes and

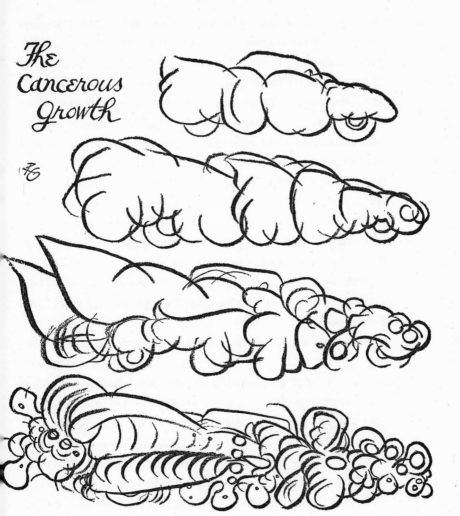

The
Cancerous
growth

intellectuals from the effete East—from the kind of people who drove Volkswagens and read highbrow magazines just to show off.

Creeping Charlie Wilsonism can best be explained in terms of General Motors' new research and development center. The building is not dedicated to true, or basic research —to development of new ideas. Rather, it is devoted to applied engineering, which is the art of placing old wine in plastic bottles. This bespeaks the dicta of Mr. Charles Wilson, former director of General Motors' destiny, who said: "Basic research is when you don't know what you're doing," and, again, "if we want to go ahead and have pure research, let us let somebody else subsidize it." Thus, the bulk of the millions that GM spends on innovation is spent on styling—on superficial detail that has nothing whatever to do with the efficiency of the product.

In styling as in engineering, however, the word is still careful sloth and General Motors is much admired in Detroit for selecting new styles which go just so far, but not too far ahead in any one year.

At this point, we should reflect that all the necessary chemistry and physics of automobile engineering were well known in 1900, and that most of the significant applications of these natural laws were completed by the mid-1930s. Yet, not all of the applications are offered as standard, or even as optional equipment today. Consider fuel-injection, for instance, now offered as an option on some automobiles. The system is no different than the one first used in German engines in 1898. The red lights on the dashboard instead of the dial gauges

The AMORPHOUS, amœboid shape! ....or....
Detroits' idea of disciplined design!

for oil pressure and battery amperage? In 1915, such lights appeared on the Detroiter automobile. The headlamps that turn with the front wheels? Here is a device that traffic safety engineers beg Detroit to install, and perhaps some day, Detroit will. It would cost General Motors nothing to find out how to do this, since the plans first appeared in the pages of *Popular Mechanics* magazine in 1907. During the 1930s, electric starters, hydraulic brakes, demountable wheels, all-steel bodies, safety glass and automatic windshield wipers were with us, and the only wonder of it all is why they were so long in arriving, and why, for example, the windshield wipers on a $4,900 automobile are still apt to fall off. Apart from Detroit's lack of originality and imagination, the answer is bound up in our third reason for delay—to maintain a high price for a used car.

I take it we all agree the entire economy of the greatest nation on earth spins around the automobile. Just in case you don't take it, I'm going to give it to you anyway. Detroit is our biggest consumer of coal, iron, steel, plate glass, radios, rubber, many kinds of plastics, and other little odds and ends. If Detroit can't sell its wares, Detroit won't buy the raw materials and hire the workers, and people will be out of work not only in Detroit, but also nearly everywhere else, because of the interdependent nature of our technological society.

This means, of course, that Detroit must somehow keep on producing automobiles forever, a matter involving some risk. If, for example, Detroit made unbreakable automobiles of an excellent standard design, Detroit would soon produce enough to saturate the market. Nobody would ever need another car,

and Detroit would have put itself out of business. With that rare vision which so often characterizes the American business mind, Detroit's answer was to build what General Motors executives call "dynamic obsolescence" into its products. In English translation, "dynamic obsolescence" means that Detroit thinks this year's car is guaranteed to become so unstylish in four years that you won't be able to stand the sight of the thing.

The critical factor, or element in our compound, is the controlled speed of the decay. The average dealer sells 150 new cars and 225 used cars each year. He must accept a used car in partial payment on a new car purchase because the new cars are fantastically expensive and taking the old car in trade helps the customer to imagine he can really afford a new debt. If the dealer does not wish to enter voluntary bankruptcy, he must sell both new and used cars at a profit. The manufacturing trick therefore becomes one of bringing out a car just a little different each year, but not too different, so as to allow a proper time for this year's dreamboat to become another year's dog, without a sudden drop in price in the meantime. In other words, Detroit must combine creeping Charlie Wilsonism with the Barnum Law of economics, while allowing the customer to pay for everything. Detroit calls this "cycling"; the normal period is three years, and this is how it's done at General Motors, according to *Fortune* magazine:

For its 50-some models, General Motors has three basic shells, or bodies, which it forthrightly calls A, B and C. The basic A bodies are used by both Chevrolet and Pontiac divisions. B bodies go on the Oldsmobiles, and on the Buick Special and Century models. The C bodies fit the Cadillacs, Buick Roadmasters and Supers. The idea is to leave A body alone this year; do some tinkering with B and bring out a radically different C. Next year, you leave C alone, trifle with A; bring out new B. The third year, you introduce new A, leave B untouched; tinker with C. The cycle is now complete —it's Detroit's version of the shell game.

This little dance is as stylized as a Balinese *legong,* because all General Motors cars must also have what the trade calls a "family resemblance." In General Motors' case, the basic presumption is that whatever the Cadillac looks like is beautiful, because the Cadillac is the most expensive car in the family. Therefore, the more a car looks like a Cadillac, and the closer it comes to the Cadillac's price, the more beautiful it is. Therefore, all General Motors cars must look like apprentice, or junior-grade Cadillacs. Furthermore, all General Motors cars must tell the purchaser on sight: (1) the model year (2) that it is a General Motors car (3) that it is the product of a certain General Motors division (4) that it is descended from last year's model produced by that division and (5) that it won't look too much different two years from now than the Cadillac of today.

What is true of styling is also true of mechanical changes in the General Motors family. For example, General Motors introduced the hardtop in 1948, the vision-distorting wraparound windshield in 1954, and Europe's old air springs in 1957. General Motors' genius in the timing of its sea changes is the despair of its imitative competitors. As the Ford company's Edsel people told *Harper's* magazine in September, 1957, "There's hardly anything we're doing that GM hasn't done. They know their business and a sweet-running business it is. We're just trying to catch up." But, also hewing to the dictates of creeping Charlie Wilsonism, the Edsel people aren't trying too hard—just hard enough.

Perhaps because General Motors sells more cars in America than all other manufacturers, foreign and domestic, it is somehow inevitable that General Motors should set the pace in both engineering and styling. Since, as we have seen, General Motors is not interested in original engineering, changes in that area are slow to arrive on the market. As Mr. George Romney, president of American Motors, points out, General Motors and "every other company is still building cars with the construction methods used to build oxcarts and buggies."

Likewise, the three-year crawl of the General Motors cycle prevents the instantaneous adoption of a radically new style, for if all General Motors cars must somewhat resemble the Cadillac, it must be said that other manufacturers seem constrained to build things that look something like the Cadillac, too.

Thus, since engineering is a dead duck, or at least a duck in the advanced stages of rigor mortis, and since styling changes must be minute and slow to arrive, automotive progress in America today boils down to this:

The basic steel shell is bent a little bit this way, this year, and is bent slightly that way next year. The headlights are higher one year, lower the next, or grow in double, either side by side or one atop the other, or on the bias. The door knobs are hidden, or recessed, or turned into buttons or bars, and the chromium stripes are shifted about a bit here and a bit there from one year to another. Grilles grow massive or "classical." Tail fins grow higher, or may be, grow in side-wise. A chiropodist has remarked the Edsel's fins resemble ingrown toenails.

Rigor Mortis

Meanwhile, no significant changes take place, except in price, and the change there is certainly significant. Indeed, the graph of automobile prices in recent years is a nearly vertical line. Otherwise automotive progress is imperceptible when seen from year to year, but from the vantage of several years, one can easily see that it is a slow parabola tending ever farther into the realms of outer whimsy.

Finally, we see the mechanic's rude observation of the love life of the American automobile is just; it is borne out by the investigations of more sophisticated minds. David Ogilvy, president of an advertising agency, notes "there isn't any significant difference" among American automobiles, any more than among cake mixes or detergents. Thus, Mr. Loewy says every company produces "imitative, overdecorated chariots, with something for everyone laid over a basic formula design that is a copy of someone else's formula design." We have entered a period of design that is a kind of Egyptian stylization overlaid with Persian curlicues.

The weak glue that holds Detroit together is therefore compounded of dynamic obsolescence—although "dynamic" seems hardly the *mot juste* that describes the pace of Detroit's minute changes—of the sale of used cars, and of something called the installment plan. The role of the used car and the implications of the installment plan are matters we will investigate in some detail in another chapter. Suffice it to say now that the American economy is curiously predicated on the hope that a man who can't afford to buy a decaying automobile will, nevertheless, buy one, and that the automobiles are all headed for the junk heap at a predetermined speed.

I am painfully aware that I have not supplied a satisfactory answer to the question of whether it is Detroit or the public that makes our automotive taste. Nearly all Americans have convinced themselves that they each need an automobile—a proposition as open to question as the theory that since everyone drinks milk, everyone should keep a cow. Since Americans must generally buy from Detroit, buy they do, so it doesn't seem to make much difference what Detroit sees fit to produce—the public will be stuck with it in any case. On the other hand, a large part of the public does seem to want fripperies, as any dealer will tell you, and so we can say Detroit has this fact in mind.

Perhaps we come closer to the truth when we say there is an interaction here, and we can understand it better when we realize that Detroit does not produce cars for reasonable people like thee and me, but for that vast section of the American public that presumably has something radically wrong with it. If our cars are only minutely different, perhaps this bespeaks the fact that little things loom large in little minds. At all events, every automobile advertisement tells the reasonable man that the advertisement was written for someone suffering from a serious character defect, and it is not surprising to discover that this is true in literal fact. The wording is deliberate, and the car described is deliberately designed for the nut that is eventually to hold the wheel. If Detroit is right in this matter, there is little wrong with the American car that is not wrong with the American public. Now this is quite an assumption, but it is the one upon which Detroit has built its shabby fortunes, as the next chapter will disclose.

THE AD AND THE ID

KING FAROUK had—and for all I know still has—an automobile horn that imitates the squeals and howls of dogs being mangled under his wheels,* and society's offhand judgment of this royal lump of suet is that he's as crazy as a suit of red flannels hung on a clothesline in a high wind. Before we dash off to the Riviera with a canvas shirt, however, we might want to try it on for size ourselves, because Detroit builds and sells us automobiles on the theory that we are just as daft as Farouk.

The Buick Company, for instance, says that driving a Buick "makes you feel like the man you are"—which is just another way of saying we can't distinguish between illusion and reality, but that buying a Buick will create in our misty minds the *illusion* that we *really are* what we *really are*. Other manufacturers entertain an equally thin view of us—with result that

---

* So *Holiday* magazine reports.

automobiles are not marketed as reliable machines for reasonable men to use, but as illusory symbols of sex, speed, wealth and power for daydreaming nitwits to buy.

It must be said that Detroit didn't just make all these assumptions up out of thin air. Ever its own worst enemy, the American public has said time and again that it doesn't care beans about sweet reason whenever it steps into an automobile showroom. Dealers say that less than three per cent of new car buyers look under the hoods, and fewer still ask specific questions as to construction, reliability and performance.

"A guy comes in and he looks at the shape, and that's all," a Buick dealer told the author. "Nobody wants to know how it's made or why it runs, or even if it runs.

"But then," the dealer sighed, "it wouldn't do 'em any good even if you told 'em, because the way they're building cars these days, it takes one specialist to find the choke and another specialist to fix it.

"Besides," he confided, "all the cars today work about the same, and they all last about as long. A guy's a fool if he doesn't just go out and buy the cheapest one there is."

Well, the number of fools among us ranges between 87.9 and 93.9% of the population, according to *Popular Mechanics* magazine, which in February, 1956, interviewed 10,000 people to try to find out who buys what car for what reason.

The statistics make fascinating reading for anyone with a taste for harlequinade. They build a profile of the average American automobile buyer, and if you think this country is a land of hard-headed, no-nonsense Yankee traders, you can start unthinking it right away. For instance, *Popular Mechanics'* average man owns a car that works perfectly well at the moment. There is no good reason to turn it in. He does turn it in, however, lamely explaining that he "just wanted a new one."

Next, we find a strong pattern of irrationality running through our average man's explanation for buying the particular kind of new car that he buys. For example, even if he owns to his need for a smaller car, he says he won't buy one.

Why? Because, *Popular Mechanics* says, the average man says if he makes a little more money next year, he'll buy a bigger car with it.

Popular Mechanics said the largest single percentage—25.3% of all new car buyers—will buy the same make from year to year. An even larger percentage will buy within the same manufacturing family. For instance, this year's Chevrolet

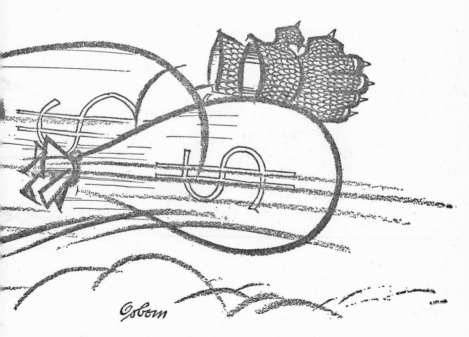

owner will probably buy next year's Chevrolet, or he might buy next year's Buick—for both are made by General Motors. He is not at all likely to jump from his General Motors Chevrolet to a Ford or Chrysler Corporation product. One reason why the customer sticks with one manufacturer all his buying life is his belief—often well founded—that he'll get a bigger trade-in allowance on his old Chevrolet, say, if he buys a new Chev than if he traded for a Ford. Nevertheless, some customers buy from the same manufacturer year after year even when dealers for other manufacturers are offering bigger trade-in allowances. Such customers are simply slaves to habit, if not slightly psychopathic. Detroit prefers to regard them as "loyal." In any event, there's every indication the average man most usually will not only patronize the same manufacturer forever, but that he will also completely ignore all other manufacturers, *no matter what they are offering. Popular Mechanics* added that most of the buyers who said they'd be willing to look at another manufacturer's wares are uninterested in engineering, operation or price—that their comparisons are made solely on superficial appearance.

Popular Mechanics' survey showed that price ranked fourth among primary reasons for purchase. First came "family loyalty"; next came turn-in value (which is assumed for most customers to be bound up in the first reason); then came styling. Family loyalty aside, "it seems that styling, or exterior appearance, is the most important influence in the choice of a new car," the magazine reported. Of all who buy a new model of the car they drive, only 12.1% think first in terms of price, the magazine said. Of those who buy a new car of a different

make, only 6.1% consider price first. Handling ease, performance, cost of operation and engineering lagged even farther
than price behind superficial appearance as primary reasons
for the sale.*

In sum, *Popular Mechanics'* study indicates the average
American changes cars for change's sake, buys from the same
company simply because he's bought from it before, equates
size with value and makes his choice on the least practical
feature of his purchase. This quaint custom, *Popular Mechanics* said, is pretty much the same for all income groups.

Interestingly enough, the magazine's average man earns between $5,000 and $10,000 a year, and yet he dreams of buying a Cadillac. Thirty-nine and a half per cent of our average
men lust after Cadillacs, *Popular Mechanics* said, and this
percentage is greater than the combined percentages of those
who would next settle (in order of choice) for Lincolns,
Chryslers and Oldsmobiles, given the money. Here is substantial evidence that General Motors' theory is correct that the
more a car looks like a Cadillac, the greater its chance in the
market place.

Ordinarily, you might think Detroit could build a pretty
good sale on the basis of such studies; that Detroit would accept the reasons people give for buying as the real reasons for
the sale. For example, let's say we agree that styling is what

---

* It is interesting to note that turn-in value looms so large in buyers'
minds. A man may get a bigger turn-in price from Dealer A than from
Dealer B, yet wind up paying much more for the new car bought from
Dealer A than he would have paid Dealer B. It would seem many customers
count only the dollars they're "allowed" on a car they're throwing away,
and fail to count the dollars they spend on the car they're buying.

sells the car. So, being a reasonable fellow, you say the car with the best style will enjoy the best sale. It naturally occurs to you to wonder what style that might be. If you happen to think the best form of anything is that which most closely fits the function to be served, you are being quite reasonable. You will also never get a job in Detroit, because Detroit takes a negative view of the evidence. Detroit thinks (a) that men are not reasonable and (b) since they are not reasonable, the reasons they give cannot be their real reasons for buying. In this case, when a man says he's buying style, Detroit says he doesn't mean a style related to mechanical function, because he isn't really talking about an automobile in the first place. We can see this best by taking a close look at the Cadillac, the average man's dreamboat:

General Motors tells us the newest Cadillac "Eldorado Brougham" has "anti-dive control, a power train, outriggers, pillarless styling, projectile-shaped gull-wing bumpers, outboard exhaust ports, four metal magnetized gold-finish drinking cups, [a bottle of] perfume, an antenna which automatically rises to urban height, ventipanes [and a] sound wave opening for the horn."

This contraption is more than eighteen feet long, and more than six and a half feet wide, but it has only five and three-tenths inches road clearance—and once you're inside it, you discover there is less than one yard from the seat to the ceiling, and only 43.7 inches allowed—at most—for your legs.

Now let's try to examine our dreamboat from a rational point of view, beginning with an attempt at English translation:

The name implies this is a light, closed carriage that comes to us from an imaginary land abounding in gold. The carriage has "anti-dive control" which apparently means that something prevents it from not diving. A "sound wave opening for the horn" permits the horn's noise to escape. The image of a projectile shaped like a gull's wing, or a gull's wing shaped like a projectile, is not for the rational mind to grasp. One wonders what is meant by "urban height"—presumably it means the average height of all cities. One also wonders why a light carriage from a golden land should have both a powerful train and outriggers attached to it. Only when one comes to outboard exhaust ports does something fall sweetly on the ear. One can see the good sense for this, for one can readily imagine how difficult ordinary respiration would become were the exhaust pipes to empty themselves inside the car.

By and large, however, we can say the Cadillac's description of itself is not meant to be taken literally. Instead, it is designed to create the impression that the Eldorado is really not an automobile at all. It is a graceful carriage from Lord Brougham's own carriage house. Your attention is directed to the dreams of Spanish conquistadores. You are asked to think of the thundering power of the Twentieth Century Limited, of Hawaiians skimming past sunny islands in outrigger canoes, of the intimacy of milady's boudoir, of sixteen-inch naval shells, of gulls soaring and—apparently—bumping into each other. You are asked to don a white suit to enter a laboratory to measure sound waves with your fellow-physicists. All of these associations can be yours for only $13,000.

The price, like the description, implies this thing which is more than an automobile is not built for most people, and physical inspection proves it. It is a thing built for very rich, very short people who have no parking problems. Let's wander around an Eldorado and creep into it and see for ourselves.

If you can keep up a brisk pace of six feet per second, it will take you slightly more than eight seconds just to circumnavigate the Eldorado's 117 square feet, but in slightly more than one second, you have marched past all the available leg room allotted the occupants. Or, to put it another way, barely one-fifth of the Eldorado's massive 503.1 cubic feet is reserved for human habitation; only thirty-five square feet—less than one-third of the whole area—is devoted to people. In short, two-thirds, or four-fifths of the Eldorado is not concerned with the people who ride in it, depending on how you wish to compare the usable space with the over-all size.

Next, we find that a six-foot man will have only 6.2 inches' tolerance when wedged behind the wheel, because the combined number of inches of head and foot room in the front seat is only 78.2. It is therefore obvious that a six-foot man cannot wear both a hat and ripple-soled shoes at the same time and drive an Eldorado. On the other hand, the seats are five feet wide, and so we can say that a man who is five feet tall and four feet wide would have at least a foot of room in which to bob up and down, and six inches to sway from side to side.

Suppose, now, that we are going to fill the Eldorado with six small, skinny people. They sit three in front and three in back. One of them reaches for the perfume atomizer and puffs

Dream Boat

at a tiny ear. Applying Boyle's Law, governing the expansion of gases in a confined space, we discover that not one, but six people will immediately take on the odor of the Arpège, Extrait de Lanvin, that comes with the car, whether they like it or not.

There are other, minor contradictions about the Eldorado Brougham from the practical point of view, but we must realize that we are not dealing with practicality when we discuss dreams. It is a fact, apparently, that styling is what sells the Eldorado. It is a fact that most average men dream of owning an Eldorado. Therefore, we are tempted to presume that the Eldorado's style must be the best there is. At the same time, we are confronted with the fact that the Eldorado's style is not functional, because (among other reasons) the average man is not rich, is not short, is not fat, and he usually has parking problems. The point, however, is that we cannot compare the practical function of a machine with dreams—we must wonder whether the Eldorado is functional *as an inducer of dreams.*

The Eldorado's sales figures and the *Popular Mechanics'* statistics on the average man's lust assure us that this is indeed the case, and this being so, I now invite the American Medical Association to pay some attention to a population that wants to buy an automobile not because it is primarily an automobile, which the Eldorado certainly is not, but because it wants to buy an automobile that is primarily a combination of illusions. People who buy illusions suffer from what I will call the Cadillac Syndrome, or Texas Nexus.

Detroit is acutely aware of the prevalence of the syndrome, but regards those who suffer from it as customers, not as patients. Therefore, Detroit spends literally millions of dollars to spread the disease, and billions more to deepen the symptoms. Once again, it must be said that Detroit has sound reasons; reasons rooted in the reality of our automotive history.

The historical fact is that at no point—not even in the eminently sensible early days of the Model T—was the automobile considered primarily as a machine. In the beginning, the foreign automobile was the plaything of the rich. It didn't make much difference then what sort of car a man owned—if he owned any car at all he was presumed to be rich and he could expect to have 30% added to his bills by his butcher, his baker and his candlestick maker. A car was a status-symbol, like a boar's tusk in a Papuan's nose. Later, when automobiles became more plentiful, society drew a line between the man who owned a Locomobile and the man who owned a Ford—the bigger the tusk, the more honorable the nose. This state of affairs has endured, enabling Pierre Martineau, advertising director of the *Chicago Tribune,* to remark that the automobile "tells us who we are and what we think we want to be . . . it is a portable symbol of our personality and our . . . exact position." *

That the automobile was not only a status-symbol but also a portable symbol of the personality of the driver was also apparent in the earliest days. It was an adventurous contraption, and so it was assumed by all that the rich owner was a daredevil—an assumption the owners did nothing to correct, but rather encouraged. Early motoring costumes had a swagger about them. Goggles bespoke frightening speeds and the long duster became as well associated with desperate deeds as the trenchcoat has become the international disguise of the world's secret agents.

Even when automobiles evolved into the closed sedan, the atmosphere of adventure persisted. Speed increased and so did horsepower, and today's advertising is rife with mention of that "power when you need it"—the implication being that you must constantly be able to outrace death at any moment. Just as different automobiles came to symbolize various degrees of wealth and social position, so did they come to symbolize different degrees of foolhardiness. Society distinguishes today between the matronly passenger in a black Buick sedan and the short-haired minx who pours herself into a Chevrolet Corvette.

---

* As quoted in Mr. Vance Packard's incisive *The Hidden Persuaders,* David McKay Company, New York, 1957.

Sex, of course, never need wait to be asked to raise its lovely head, and identification of the automobile as a sexual symbol was an instantaneous reflex action for America. Even before the first playboy squeezed the bulb of his serpent horn at the first passing tart, village maidens deployed themselves at strategic intersections, pinching color into their cheeks, trusting that a goggled millionaire would shortly appear to shower them with his welcome, illegal attentions. The clergy took a dim view of this behavior, and redundantly inveighed against the "profligate young heirs" who were whisking virgins off to debauchery in their "devil wagons" at speeds ranging from 8 to 20 miles an hour. The total number of wenches tossed on back seats was at first probably no greater than that theretofore tossed in haylofts, but events marched on. More and more cars parked in lonely lanes, until a juvenile court judge was able to denounce the family car as "a house of prostitution on wheels." Southern Methodist University sociologists discovered motels renting the same cabins sixteen times a night. Mr. J. Edgar Hoover remarked that bona-fide travelers were refused at such establishments where there was "more money and a faster turnover in the couple trade."

Detroit was certainly not blind to any of this, and responded not only by putting a dream girl in every advertisement of a dreamboat, but also by building deliberate sexual symbols into automobile designs in the expectation that the car's outward shape would precisely represent the shape of the customer's sexual peculiarity. It is not sheer accident, for example, that most manufacturers put penial geegaws on the hoods of their cars, or that Cadillac's stylists speak of the "bosoms" on their bumpers, or that Buick came up with its famous ring pierced

by a flying phallus, or that Madison Avenue was quick to ap-
plaud the Edsel for its "vaginal look," or that so many Detroit stylists lavish so much attention on the rear ends of automobiles. How much of all this is appreciated by the average
conscious mind is open to serious question. What is not open
to question is the fact that Detroit believes, and operates on
the theory that Americans don't buy automobiles, but instead
buy dreams of sex, speed, power and wealth. Detroit sees one
of its little problems to be finding some way to provide everyone with his private variation of favorite illusions, while at the
same time engaging in mass production.

Detroit was helped to its conclusion by the activities of a
rather curious group of men who call themselves "motivation
research" experts and who claim to probe the depths of the
customer's subconscious mind to discover the real reasons for
his purchase. In his best-selling exposé, *The Hidden Persuaders,* Mr. Vance Packard shows us quite clearly how Detroit
accepts the advice of these psyche snoops as a means to ex-
ploit the Cadillac Syndrome. For instance, Mr. Packard says
one depth-probing agency claims to have discovered that people buy powerful cars to find an outlet for their aggressive
impulses. Buying a new and more powerful car each year or
so gives the purchaser a renewed sense of power and reassures
him of his masculinity; the purchaser can sneer at the world
while he speeds down a road.

At the same time, speeding is breaking the law. Breaking
the law summons up guilt feelings. A man who buys a car
capable of breaking the law in a rather vivid way, and who
knows this is why he's buying the car, has guilt feelings even
while he's signing the sales contract. Lest such a guilty feeling

71

interfere with a possible sale, motivation research has an answer: use a clever sales line. Don't tell the customer the thing will do 140 in reverse. Tell him instead that he's smart—he's buying that extra power he will need to save his life. According to Mr. Packard, motivation researchers say the purchaser must always be given some "illusion of reality" for buying what he buys. Thus, accepting this advice, Detroit is now busily selling delusions of grandeur to weak-minded people by cleverly offering them irrational rationalizations.

No doubt time will prove depth-probing and motivation research to be as lugubrious as Gallian phrenology—an *ex-post-facto* mumbo-jumbo—but the fact remains that nobody in Detroit cracked a smile when Ernest Dichter, president of the Institute for Motivation Research, delivered the paper that Detroit knows as "Mistress versus Wife." Once again, Mr. Packard's analysis of this document, and Detroit's reactions, is illuminating:

It seems that automobile dealers had long known it was the convertible in the show window that lured the customer into the store. The average man stared at the convertible like the elders at Susannah, and—according to Mr. Packard—Mr. Dichter chose to regard this with Viennese eyes. The convertible, Mr. Dichter explained, was the mistress such a man wants. It represents his perpetual daydream of youth and beguiling sin. He knows perfectly well he'd never have the courage, the brains or the money to keep a mistress, but he dreams his little dream anyway. Then he marches into the store and buys a plain old frump of a sedan. To such a man, the sedan represents the humdrum wife that the customer knows to be the best female bargain he has any real right to expect.

Then, suddenly, the answer to this dilemma appeared. The hardtop burst upon the market. It became the fastest-selling of all innovations and—Mr. Packard says—motivation researchers promptly claimed this was because the hardtop combined the virtues of both mistress and wife in one germ-free package. Thus, solemnly believing the depth-probers, Detroit's devout view of the people who buy hardtops is that they're really frustrated lechers whose automobiles are portable symbols of their baffled desires.

The preposterous presumptions of motivation research are equaled only by Detroit's willingness to accept them, but there's little to be gained by brooding over this state of affairs. Facts are facts, and one of the facts to consider is that Detroit believes that the cars people buy reflect the personalities of the people who buy them, because motivation research thinks so. Thus, automobiles are advertised not as machines, but as extensions of one's id. A Cadillac advertisement, for example, is predicated on the assumption that you want other people to think you have a taste for elegance, are wealthy and proud—and that you also think that other people are so foolish as to believe Cadillacs are purchased only by proud, wealthy and elegant people.

Detroit's advertising departments not only bite hard on this sort of tinsel bait, but—becoming a bit more practical—they also pay close attention to the sociological findings of Lloyd Warner. Mr. Warner is author of *The Social Class in America,* a book that divides the nation into six classes—the upper-upper, or entrenched aristocrats; the lower-upper, or nouveau riche; the upper-middle, or professional and executive class; the lower-middle, or white collar workers; the upper-lower, or skilled and semi-skilled workers, and the lower-lower class of day laborers and greenhorn foreigners.

Mr. Warner concludes that the first three classes comprise only 15% of the population, and that the lowest class equals another 20%. Thus 65% of our population consists of the upper-lower and lower-middle classes and, naturally, this represents a vast bulk of the nation's consumers. Since market research also shows that women do 80% of America's buying, it seemed obvious to Mr. Warner and to Detroit, that this "middle majority woman is the target you are supposed to hit."

National advertising usually portrays the American woman as a pretty (but not too pretty), intelligent (bright, but not brainy), well groomed (but far from chic) female (but not unduly macromastiac) engaged in some interesting (but not unusual) situation. Such advertising is just throwing fish to the seals, because the fact, naturally, is that the majority of our womenfolk fall into the upper-lower or lower-middle classes, and hence are apt to be somewhat paunchy, mentally myopic drabs with straight hair. This Judy O'Grady, Mr. Warner adds, works harder than the Colonel's Lady, keeps a dull routine, is happy only with familiar things and tends to view the world outside her cage as dangerous and threatening. "Her imaginative resources are highly limited," Mr. Warner says. "And this is very important. Her emotional life is highly restricted and repressed, spontaneity is very low, she has a strong moral code that presses in on her most of the time, and she feels a deep sense of guilt when she deviates from it."

Whether Mr. Warner is correct in his assumptions is absolutely unimportant. What is important is that Detroit is spending a lot of its customers' money—yours and mine—to build a dreamboat that will be simultaneously pleasing to a lecherous goat and acceptable to a woman that Detroit privately envisions as a dull, repressed, unimaginative, blowsy fright.

Thus, we now begin to see why Ford Motor Company's Mr. Walker tells us that he's spent millions of dollars to find a floor covering that duplicates the rug in the average woman's living room.

Thus, we learn at last the real reason why a farmer can no longer buy a truck that looks like a truck, but must instead buy something with chrome trim, white sidewall tires, and quilted upholstery. The thing isn't designed to carry a pig to market—it's designed to please Detroit's vision of a hayseed's goody.

Thus, we now understand why the Chevrolet Division of General Motors hired seven psychologists to investigate the effect of the Chevrolet's *sounds and smells*. The head-feelers reported; the report was translated into action in the design department; the result was that in 1957, Chevrolet's general manager could proudly claim, "We've got the finest door-slam this year we've ever had—a big car sound." In short, Chevrolet had created an illusion of value with a sound; an illusion to sell to a daydreaming, uncritical mind all come down with manifestations of the Cadillac Syndrome.

Life in Detroit must take on magic hues when the problems become so involved. Imagine what fun it must be to be a Detroit designer, and know that you have to design a symbol of aggressive masculinity for the man, and at the same time contrive to keep the contraption from outraging the sensibilities of the repressed nag whose opinion will probably determine the sale.

How do you market something that is a symbol of speed, sex, wealth and power to Pop when it must also appear unimaginative, unspontaneous, routine and unexciting for Mom?

Detroit's answer to date is that you, as a designer, need not do anything well. First, you start out with a basic shape—an oblong over four wheels, with a smaller oblong on top, like a matchbox on a shoebox. You do not depart from this basic pattern lest you trend into the area of the unique and the unfamiliar. Then, you put breast-shaped bumps on the bumpers and a gaudy stern on the thing to titillate Pop. You shove Mom's rug inside. You load the car with enough power to make Pop think he's the Four Horsemen of the Apocalypse, and you put a plastic pad on the dashboard to let Mom know she won't crack her skull when the power brakes catch.

You do not need to depend entirely on the findings of the depth-probers to help you design a car's symbolism, sounds and smells, although you must of course pay some attention to their words. But there are many things about the average man you can notice for yourself. For instance, there are the conspicuous consumers, or Texans. There are the antique car collectors and the sports car enthusiasts. Ask yourself how these people relate to the average man. Your job will be to adopt from the eccentricities of these defectives because the average man is susceptible to the Cadillac Syndrome, or illusion chasing, as much as they are. His illness differs only in degree.

For example, there is no basic difference between the Ohio

teen-ager who ties a $1 Rebel flag to his antenna and Lady Nora Docker, who paid Hooper & Co., the London coach-makers, $100,000 to furnish her Daimler with gold brocade that matched her Paris frock of the moment, and to add a gold-edged Wedgwood tea service, gold teaspoons, a man's toilet kit, a woman's vanity set, and gold-chased silver vacuum bottles to the paraphernalia in the back seat. The difference is simply a superficial $99,999.00.

Similarly, there is no real difference between the man who orders chromium door-edge guards for his coupé and Lady Nora's demand that seven thousand six-pointed gold stars adorn her Daimler's flanks, and that every bit of exposed metal, from ignition key to exhaust pipe, be gold-plated. There is also no difference between the man who thinks of a car in terms of a big, empty luggage compartment and Lady Nora, who asked Hooper & Co. to furnish, also, a fitted alligator-skin luggage trunk with gold clasps. Likewise, there is no difference between the man who, living on a bus route, maintains two automobiles and the Texan who orders a seventeenth pink Cadillac to fill an empty space in his eighteen-Cadillac garage.

As a Detroit designer, you should therefore be aware that the most prevalent form of the Cadillac Syndrome is conspic-uous consumption. Hence, your first consideration is that your ultimate design be both lavish and largely useless, but since you want to sell as many cars as possible—no matter how much you'd like to design something just for imaginative Lady Nora—you cannot be too extravagant. You must create the *illusion* that your lavish automobile has real value. Thus, when you build the Eldorado Brougham, you do not use real kara-kul rugs; you use "high-pile nylon Karakul." When you fit out the Ford station wagon, you do not use leather upholstery, but an imitation made of plastic. You are aided in your work by your heritage, for the American genius has ever been to make the shoddy seem genuine.

As a Detroit designer, you must also be aware of the presence of odd balls among us. To be sure, the antique automobile collector is often a bore, as collectors are often apt to be, but still he has something to offer you. Because he is an eccentric, he is often regarded as news by national magazines. Hence, at any jaded moment his eccentricities may be blown up into national fads. He is always talking about "classic" shapes. The average man is apt to be impressed by the closed code the antique car collector uses as a language. As a designer, you must capitalize on this. Recall to your mind the long, narrow, useless shape of an ancient hood and radiator. Stick an adaption of it on your newest dreamboat and beat your breast and cry out that your car, and yours alone, has the "classic shape" of the fabled limousines of a bygone era. The average man is just as susceptible to personification, anthropomorphism and deification as the collector—it's just that he doesn't have the money or the discrimination to indulge his fancies. Help him.

Likewise, as a Detroit designer, you must certainly be aware of the curious ways, speech and costumes of the sports car set. Like blue-water yachtsmen, inveterate foxhunters, dog breeders and polo players, sports car fanciers lead a narrow life, wear funny hats, and speak a closed code, too, but they are nonetheless envied by the average clod who has the will, but not the means to join in their rallies. So you must add a suggestion of a sports car to your overblown dreamboat with its sexuality, its lavishness, and its classical lines. A clock that looks like a tachometer will do the trick. Nobody knows what the word tachometer means, or what the instrument does, or having done it, what happens next, but sports cars have tachometers, so stick a clock that looks like one on that Christmas tree you've built for a dashboard and advertise a "panel with sports car styling."

As a Detroit designer, you go on and on, putting curlicue on curlicue, adding dream to dream, adding the fragment of one illusion to the fragment of another and you spend enough money to operate a state university to imitate the sound of a slammed door. When you're all through, you discover that you've transformed a rolling shoebox into a combination of the Blue Grotto and the Crystal Palace, wherein is placed a psychiatrist's couch that has enough Procrustean potential to suit any psyche, no matter how warped.

Lights wink on and off inside and outside your masterpiece and the atmosphere surrounding your rolling shebeen may be heavy with the scent of one standard brand of perfume. Whatever it is that you have made cannot be called a motor car, as the Army peep, for instance, can reasonably be called a motor car. What you have made defies description for the simple reason that it is not designed to be any one thing, but an agglomeration of constituent elements of unrelated dreams. Following directions, you have created a device to sell to a not-too-bright population sick with the Cadillac Syndrome, and you depend on your advertising and sales departments to spread and deepen the disease, which will inevitably add to your future personal problems.

If women were as grotesque as American cars

If men were as barbarous as American cars

4

"SOUNDS LIKE 'DEAD CELL'"
—The Game

WHEN in the course of human events it seemed necessary to the Ford Motor Company to bring forth on this continent a brand-new motor car to be called the Edsel, care was taken that the American populace was not uninformed of the company's intentions. Ford's advertising campaign hewed to the same dispassionate standards that have distinguished it since the day it proclaimed the first Fordmobile to be "Boss of the Road. The latest and best. It is positively the most perfect machine on the market, having overcome all drawbacks such as smell, noise, jolt, etc., common to all other makes of Auto Carriages."

The time—the fall of 1957—could not have been more propitious for the introduction of a basically new automobile, because 1957 was the end of an era. Detroit seems not to have noticed it, but the nation in that year was beginning to look for new values of every kind, having begun to emerge from a decade of noisy, glittering drift that was itself a reaction to the prior years of depression and war. During the years 1947–57, the nation engaged in a shapeless orgy. Wages were high, employment was at record levels, nobody wished to think of yesterday, and everyone seemed ready to believe that every tomorrow would be bigger and better and twice as yummy. The pursuit of happiness seemed to be the nation's single-minded intent, and although there were plenty of people who understood that every action contains its own reaction, it was hopefully suggested by practically all hands that the reaction, if any, would take place at some vague, future time, if at all. Ironically enough, it was a Russian rocket that brought most of the nation back to earth.

A dissection of the decade is not the proper concern of this volume, however. It is enough for our purposes to note that, in the fall of 1957, prior to the Red's rocket glare, more and more people were leaving the carnival to return to the main-stream of civilization. They were beginning to listen to serious men who were questioning the shape of our cities, the value of conformity, the prevailing know-nothing philosophy of the public schools, the nation's true role in world affairs and—among a thousand other things—the meaning of our automobiles. There was already a cloud no bigger than a Volkswagen on Detroit's horizon.

It was into this climate, so ripe for change, that the Ford Company introduced its Edsel. Not only was the time exactly right for something really new, but there was also no company in a better position to bring new wares to the market place. Sales of foreign cars were proceeding briskly; people were waiting as long as nine months for Volkswagen deliveries. Sales of American makes were slipping; already Detroit was cutting production. Nevertheless, General Motors, Ford and Chrysler still owned 95% of the American market, but of these companies, only Ford could gamble the $250,000,000 necessary to bring out a new car. General Motors saw no reason to change a formula that had won it nearly 50% of the market. Chrysler was committed to its then-current line of dreamboats. American Motors was trying to worm its way to the top of the remaining 5% of the market with an automobile that was a compromise between the small foreign car and the smallest of the Detroit dreamboats.* Studebaker-Packard was in dire straits. Only Ford, under eager young administration, had the money, the facilities and the desire to bring out a really new American automobile, the latest and the best, having none of the disadvantages that so distinguished all other makes.

If Ford had actually done so, its preliminary ten-million-dollars' worth of Edsel advertising would not have been necessary. Such was that public mood in the fall of 1957 that, if Ford had unveiled the first Edsel in dead silence on a lonely county crossroads at midnight, every literate child in the land would have been aware of the event ten minutes later. If, that is, the Edsel had in fact been a really new automobile. As this is written, nearly a year after the Edsel's arrival, the Edsel's qualified failure seems to be reasonably well established from

---

* Later, in the early months of 1958, it succeeded.

Detroit

a sales viewpoint. We might wonder why. Wondering, we might find some additional light to shed on that murkiest of all questions, to which there seems to be no one good answer, Does the public, or does Detroit, make taste?

There seem to be two reasons why Ford missed the boat. First, it is apparently impossible today to bring out a new car overnight, and second, nobody at the Ford plant cared about Tom Wretch. Now, the only reason why Detroit can't bring out a new automobile tomorrow is because none of Detroit's three giant corporations have any vestige of old Henry Ford's iron-headed courage, or obstinacy. When Henry was finally made to see that his Model T had run its course, he closed his plants and didn't come back into the market until he had his Model A to offer. Henry took a chance, but there don't seem to be any chance-takers in the automobile business any more—there are just wrong guessers whose bets are hedged.

As for not caring about Tom Wretch, there's a pity. Tom is the living proof that statistics can be misleading. Contrary to all the studies of buying habits, Tom does think of price first and he buys the cheapest car he can. The hidden persuaders' efforts are largely wasted on him because he buys what he must, and he has almost no depths to probe, anyway. He is dimly aware of the currents of his time, however, and his questioning of prices and values has led him to wonder why he can't find a cheap, sturdy, reliable, safe, economical automobile. We'll learn a lot more about Tom in the near future, but let's first find out why the Ford Company introduced in 1957 an automobile conceived in 1948.

Let's pretend that you and I want to manufacture an auto-

The Public

mobile. It just so happens that we already have a nationwide chain of dealers and service agencies. We have huge factories and foundries. We own a large proportion of many of the necessary raw materials, such as ore, and we have sub-assembly plants, our own ships, trains and trucks. We have thousands of well-trained blue- and white-collar workers, designers, engineers, brokers and salesmen. We have an excellent, world-wide reputation. We also happen to have a quarter of a billion dollars to blow on a new venture. All this is quite lucky for us, because no one less well equipped could think of going into the automobile business.

Question: What kind of car shall we make, and to whom shall we sell it?

In seeking answers, we thoughtfully consider the automobile's place in American life. The first, most obvious fact is that almost everyone drives, or owns a car, and that almost everyone else imagines he should. That being the case, it seems that our market is wide open, and our problem will be to make a car to sell to as many people as possible, preferably, to sell at least one of our cars to every family in America.

Next, we wonder what we can offer, specifically, that will make our car more desirable than anybody else's car, and so induce every buyer to at least *think* of our car first. We size up the current models on the road, and conclusions immediately spring to mind.

First, most cars are so expensive that people are going years into debt to buy them. Therefore, it might be desirable to undersell the market and make our profit on volume. This has also the added virtue of being a patriotic act, because going into debt is unhealthy for the individual, and a nation of debtors is a sick nation.

Second, automobiles are obviously dangerous, because each year they kill more than 40,000 Americans—the population of a middle-sized city—badly wound a million more, cause $1,100,000,000 worth of property damage and cause another $1,700,000,000 to be paid out annually in wage losses, medical expenses and insurance. Therefore, we want to build as safe a contraption as we can possibly devise, both because of our humanitarian impulses and because of a desire to offer something different that will help us make money.

Third, we notice that our cities are becoming more and more congested, and that parking is becoming more difficult, and so we will want to offer the public a car that is shorter and easier to park, both as a personal and as a public favor.

Fourth, we notice that other manufacturers are making cars that are increasingly expensive to repair and operate. Thus, our car will be simple to repair and will easily work on the cheapest fuels.

If we go on thinking in this way, we'll come up with a car the like of which Detroit has yet to see.* Since we have the plant, the time and the money, all we need to make our ideas reality is a courageous faith in the essential common decency and good sense of the American public.

The trouble with this kind of reasoning is that it is unfair, because it is the kind of thinking more and more people began to turn to in the post-Sputnik winter of 1958, and we can't

---

* Mr. Romney's American Motors, however, seems to be working in the right direction here.

say now that this was the kind of thinking that should have occurred to the Ford Motor Company in 1948, when the public mood was quite different, and when the Ford Forward Products Planning Committee began work—that was to culminate in the Edsel. All we can fairly say is that our kind of thinking did not enter the minds of the Ford company in 1948, and because it did not, Ford lost a magnificent opportunity in 1957.

The mood of 1948 was generally orgiastic, as noted, and that of the Ford company was optimistic. Well before the end of World War II, Ford had been losing a fantastic amount of money each year, but when Henry Ford II took over the seasick corporation, profound changes were wrought not only in factory conditions and pricing methods, but also in the quality of the wares. Young Henry, as the second Henry Ford was known, raided General Motors Corporation for ideas and talent, and General Motors' methods of production, cost accounting and design were installed at the Ford plants. The result, of course, was just another General Motors Corporation on a smaller scale.

One of Young Henry's concerns was to establish a "family" of cars akin to the family of Chevrolets, Buicks, Pontiacs, Oldsmobiles and Cadillacs. Ford had three cars—the Ford, the Mercury and the Lincoln. While the 1949 Ford began to compete with Chevrolet in the low price field, the Mercury was less than quicksilver in the middle bracket and the Lincoln was not at all competitive with the Cadillac. Thus, one of the Ford company's decisions was to create a line that would not only compete with the General Motors family in all respects, but also a family that would have as recognizable a family relationship as General Motors cars enjoy. This meant making sure that just as the Chevrolet bore some resemblance to the Cadillac, so the Ford products must be generally alike. It also meant either that the price ranges of all three Ford cars must be widened by use of more, slightly different models of each of the three makes, or that a new, middle car be introduced to help Mercury cover the competitive ground between the highest priced Chevrolet and the lowest priced Cadillac; specifically to compete with the highly successful Buick. Ford's Forward Products Planning Committee was handed the problem, and it came up with a six-volume answer in 1955, the gist of which was, "build another medium-priced car."

Note that there was no indication that the Ford company considered the idea of building something new to sell to as many people as possible. The view was of a narrower market —the medium price market. Remember that the mood of 1948 was expansive; manufacturers were selling anything they could make as fast as they could make it and a car-hungry public was willingly being fleeced by unscrupulous dealers. In 1948, there was every indication that automobiles could grow longer, lower, wider, more powerful and much more expensive—and the public gave every indication of being willing and able to choke down whatever was spooned out.

When Ford's Planning Committee reported in 1955, the mood was still expanding. It was the gaudiest sales year in automotive history. On the basis of market research, the extrapolation was made that, by 1965, one-half of all American families would be earning $5,000 a year; that the middle car

91

market would increase to 60% of the total market; that there would be 20,000,000 more automobiles on the road. It thus seemed reasonable to Ford's planners that, of those who bought middle-priced cars, at least 3½% could be persuaded to buy a new Ford brand, and since 3½% of the middle market was a profitable figure, the decision was made to wedge a new car into this middle market. No claim was made that the middle-car-buyer was crying his baby blue eyeballs out for something really *new;* the idea was simply that there was 3½% worth of room in the market for *another* car.

Whereupon a clutch of Columbia University depth-probers and motivation researchers was called in, and in their arbitrary way, the social scientists interviewed 1,600 unsuspecting citizens in Peoria, Illinois, and San Bernadino, California. (Why places like Peoria and San Bernadino seem to invite this sort of thing is beyond the scope of our argument. Apparently, they are believed to represent a kind of All-America rock bottom.) In the cant of their trade, the depth-probers were after "image intensity." They wanted to know if the people's images of their cars compared with the images they had of themselves, and the findings were next used to build an "image" of the car that was to become the Edsel. The images were measured on three scales—sex, age and social class.

The results alleged to show that Peorians and San Bernardinians thought that a lower class of people bought Mercuries than bought Fords; that while a middle-class Ford owner might want to step up to a bigger, more expensive car, he would consider a Mercury a step down, and he didn't—or couldn't—step two steps up to a Lincoln. The good burghers were believed to have thought Mercuries were for young light-weights, such as jazz-band leaders, while Buicks, Pontiacs, and Dodges were for the elderly. Mercuries were believed to be purchased by men, while it was thought women bought Dodges and Pontiacs. The probed citizenry figured Pontiacs, Dodges and Mercuries were bought by working-class people, while Buicks and Oldsmobiles were watchfobs of the well-to-do.

Therefore, Ford's market researchers decided, the new car would be for the young, but not too young; for the kind of people who indefinitely think of themselves as the young married set. It would be for the man who was almost well-to-do; who imagined he might one day actually become the kind of man who could buy a Buick. The new car should not have sex —that is, it shouldn't be thought of as a car women would buy, nor as a car that only men would buy. It should be, said Ford's chief of research, "the smart car for the younger executive or professional *family* on its way up." This is the reason the Edsel's advertising said "They'll know you've arrived" when you drive up in an Edsel, and why the pictures showed a middle-class family in its late thirties arriving at a middle-class house in a middle-class suburban Never-Never Land.

Instead of thinking about what a new automobile design should or could be, Ford merely thought in terms of a specific product to fit Ford's view of a specific consumer market.

At this point, there was still a chance for Ford to have done something more or less reasonable. Despite the narrow view of a product for a market, Ford could also have tried to make that product safe, simple, and cheap to operate and maintain. You would normally not think *that* too much to ask for the

93

quarter of a billion dollars Ford was ready to sink into the new product. Unfortunately, those terms did not comprise the frame of reference of 1955. Decisions relating to the Edsel were made on other grounds.

It will be remembered that one basic concept of Ford's postwar recovery was to create a family of cars analagous to General Motors'. It will also be remembered that Detroit is congenitally opposed to sudden change. Thus, the new car could not be *too* different, and, as far as possible, its parts should be interchangeable with those of other cars in the family. Thus it was that the two smaller Edsels would use the basic body of the Ford Fairlane series; the two larger Edsels would use basic Mercury bodies and components. The "new" Edsel engines would merely be Ford and Mercury engines, rebored to different dimensions. Because of the many interchangeable parts, Ford, Mercury and Edsel dealers would be able to give service to all three makes. Thus it was that while Ford was claiming to have sunk $250,000,000 into introducing the Edsel, Ford was actually hedging its bets. The "new" Edsel factory was the old Ford Continental factory with a new name on the door—the familiar scene of a prior mistake. (Two years earlier, some readers may recall, Ford decided to produce a super-luxury car, to be called the Continental, designed to out-sparkle the most sparkling Cadillac. But even in lush 1955, the market wouldn't bear the weight. The Continental was a fiscal flop of no mean proportion.) If the Edsel proved a similar fiasco, Ford could still recover $150,-000,000 by using Edsel facilities and parts to make Fords and Mercuries, just as Continental equipment was absorbed by

Lincoln. The remaining $100,000,000 could presumably be charged off to future Ford and Mercury customers. Meantime, all the Fords, Thunderbirds, Edsels, Mercuries and Lincolns would look somewhat alike, and when it came to choosing a generic style, the company chose the low rectangle of its sports car, the Thunderbird, the most blatant and least practical of its products.

The Edsel's basic design and production decisions having been made, the Ford Company next faced up to the problem of a name. Ask any advertising man, "What's in a name?" "Money," he'll say. Since the Ford company wanted to make money, several dozen of the highest paid brains in the world smoked and burst as they considered the gigantic problem of finding the magic, money-making name for what was essentially to be a car specifically designed to be sold to mediocre people. In desperation, Ford turned to the fine arts for help, enlisting the services of the poet Marianne Moore. Miss Moore, charmed and delighted, supplied a lengthy list of first-chop suggestions, including "Utopian Turtletop," but somehow even her efforts were found wanting. A middle-class man, however much he might aspire to rise, still would not aspire to Utopias.

Great ideas are often enough found right around the house, so to speak, and the longer the Ford company considered the nature of the product they had designed for a special market, the more natural it seemed to name the new creation the Edsel, after Edsel Ford, the Company's unknown middle president. If ever there was a younger executive perpetually on his way up, and never getting there, it was Edsel Ford. If ever there

95

was a middleman, sandwiched between giants, it was Edsel. He was a man overpowered and outlived by Old Henry, his father, who allowed him no real authority, and outdistanced in memory by Young Henry, his son. Moreover, the name Edsel was neither lowly, like Ed, nor royal, like Edward. It was a Texas Leaguer of a name, just as the Edsel was meant to be a Texas Leaguer of a car.

We know you will understand, the company wrote to Miss Moore, when we tell you we have decided to name the new car the Edsel.

Miss Moore doubtless understood, being a poet, and poets possess compassion. Detroit, too, understood, because everyone in that provincial city was familiar with Edsel Ford's career, and, considering the product, the name seemed no more than just. It did not occur to Detroit that perhaps no one outside the city had ever heard, or cared about Edsel Ford, because, as *Harper's* magazine pointed out, the conversations in Detroit are 75% about automobiles, 15% about sport, and 10% about last night's TV programs. Were it not for Detroit's limited *Weltanschauung,* "the selection of a name like Edsel, for a multi-million dollar investment, would have been impossible," *Harper's* said. "Their own wizards of market research, left to their own devices, would never have come up with such an answer.

" 'Look at the associations,' " *Harper's* quoted an advertising man. " 'Edsel, diesel, pretzel—Good Lord! It's a wonderful name for a plow or a tractor, but a car? They can make it elegant, but it will take them two or three years and fifty million dollars to do it.' "

96

The most the admen salvaged was the naming of the four Edsel models, which they promptly christened the Ranger, the Pacer, the Corsair and the Citation. Here were associations aplenty—and none of them were prosaic. The customer had his choice of pretending to be somehow related to the keeper of a royal forest; or to a horse of peculiar gait, or to a Barbary pirate, or of receiving an official summons to appear before a court. No doubt the Citation's name was a logical free association with its more than 300 advertised horsepower.

Conceived, designed, manufactured and named, the Edsel was now displayed and offered for trial to the press. The results were uniformly disappointing, for even such favorably inclined professional automobile writers as Tom McCahill of *Mechanix Illustrated* praised the car with faint damns. In a September, 1957 article, Mr. McCahill compared aspects of the Edsel to beasts of prey, bombardment aircraft, a music hall, boomerangs, a bag of bolts, a sausage, runaway horses and snakebites. From all reports, it was evident that the Edsel was not new, was not cheap, was not economical and was far from the safest thing on four wheels.

Let's pause for two words on this matter of safety. Each year more than 4,320,000 cubic feet of American earth is excavated to make graves for what the newspapers call our traffic victims. You'd normally think this fact would inspire some sort of action in Detroit; that it would at least lead the manufacturers into a working agreement with the nation's undertakers, if not leading perhaps one manufacturer to want to produce a somewhat safer product. Detroit's view, however, is different, because Detroit sees itself as selling nothing but dreams of speed, sex, luxury and horsepower. It would no more occur to Detroit to try to sell safety at the same time than it would occur to a fashionable restaurant to provide sodium bicarbonate and a stomach pump with every place setting.

Besides, if Detroit were to sell a safe automobile, it would have to offer a radically different car, and we have seen that Detroit loathes radical differences. A relatively safe automobile would have a well-supported, noncollapsible roof, circumferential bumpers, and no exposed metal inside the cab. The interior would be padded with collision matting; seat harnesses, not belts, would be standard equipment and the passengers would ride with their backs to the motion, so that in event of sudden stops they'd sink into padded chairs and not go flying through space to crack their pates on the windshield. A safe car would have no deep-slanted, vision-distorting wrap-around windshields; there would be dull, anti-glare paint on the unornamented hood, and the instrument panel would not glitter with chromium and leer with lights but would softly glow with ultra-violet light, as airplane instrument panels do. A safe car's wheels would be larger, to provide more braking area, instead of being made constantly smaller, with less braking area, as is now the trend with most new cars. A safe car would have its wheels at its outer corners, both for maneuverability and stability. The long, long cars that overhang their wheelbases fore, aft and amidships cannot be safely turned at speed, and they bounce like ping-pong balls when wrenched to panic halts.

None of these suggestions is either novel or impossible, but none has been adopted, despite the fact that it is faulty design that fills our graves. The National Safety Council studied 685,000 accidents in one year and discovered that 87% of them took place at 40 miles an hour or less. A Cornell University research team working with Indiana State Police estimated that of 600 fatal accidents studied, only 16% were non-survivable in any case, and that the remaining 84% of lives lost could have been saved by proper interior design. There is some evidence that you can operate an Indianapolis racer at 100 miles an hour with greater safety than a professional racing driver can operate your Detroit dreamboat at 70.

It is Detroit's contention that speed has less to do with accidents than is generally supposed; that the chief killer is bad judgment, and that the judgment of the driver is something Detroit obviously can't control. So, Detroit defends its ever-higher horsepower by saying if you have sufficient speed in reserve, you can flee from an accident before it happens. Hence the passing gear that accelerates you from 35 to 70

miles an hour in a matter of instants; hence the cars that leap to 60 miles an hour in less than ten seconds from a standing start.

All this is so much hoopla, because our automobiles are so poorly designed as to be unsafe at *any* speed, and more speed simply increases the danger. For instance, it is possible for a man to be impaled on his steering column like a bug on a pin in the course of a panic stop at 25 miles an hour. You can, at 10 miles an hour, be jerked off the front seat and lose every tooth in your skull when you fetch up on the dashboard. Furthermore, if most accidents can be attributed to bad judgment, then it would seem poor taste to supply poor judges with an opportunity to exercise their poor judgments at high speeds when there will be even less time for making any kind of decisions. Moreover, momentum equals mass times velocity, and a 3,300-pound automobile whistling along at 70 miles an hour is going to have far greater impact than the same automobile moving at 30—and so will its passengers, who go flying off the seats toward the windshield at the moment of collision. To say that most accidents occur at speeds lower than 40 miles an hour is to say nothing; it is more important to wonder how many more of the same people would have been killed in the same cars had they all been doing 80, and how many less would have died in either case had the cars been better designed against collision damage.

We should wonder about such things, because Detroit keeps building more and more powerful automobiles with higher and higher advertised speeds, while making only derisive efforts to provide safe design. In all fairness, it must be said

that the Ford Motor Company has said and done more than most companies about safety. Ford came out with the collapsible steering wheel, which is designed to bend under the pressure of your frantic, stiffened arms at the moment of impact, instead of snapping off to permit the steering column to skewer you. Ford pioneered the slow-rebound plastic padding on the dashboard and suggested that seat belts be anchored to firmly-anchored seats. At the same time, however, Ford kept on raising its speed and horsepower and provided the padding and the belts *as optional equipment available at extra cost*. Ford thus said, "Here's a hot car. Now, if you want to try to be safe in it, you'll have to pay more."

All of which brings us back to the Edsel and to our recital of missed opportunity. Given Ford's interest in safety, and given Ford's chance to produce a really new car, you'd think that Ford would have come out with the newest, safest thing on the road. So you might think. The facts are different.

Tom McCahill of *Mechanix Illustrated* wrote of the Edsel's "gigantic V-8s; the Pacer and Ranger with 361 cubic inches and the tiger-eating Corsair and Citation with an engine bigger than Carnegie Hall, displacing 410 cubic inches—at this writing the biggest automobile engines in many years. Most of my testing was done with the big bombers."

Mr. McCahill said the first fault he discovered was that he couldn't tell how fast he was going. "The revolving speedometer," he said, "develops inertia but will unquestionably be fixed before these cars are turned over to the public."

Next, it seemed "the bolt bag," as Mr. McCahill called the Edsel, had so much torque that it was impossible to give the car a "full jump start on any type of road surface, including ribbed concrete." (Why anyone would wish to give any car a full jump at any time, on any surface, is neither here nor there. The point is, if you want to, you can't with an Edsel.) "On ribbed concrete," Mr. McCahill wrote, "every time I shot the throttle to the floor quickly, the wheels spun like a gone-wild Waring Blendor. The car has enough starting torque to yank the Empire State Building off its foundations.

"At high speeds, especially through rough corners, I found the suspension a little too horsebacky," Mr. McCahill continued in his metaphorical way. "In other words," he explained, "it galloped when I didn't want it to gallop and was far too soft a ride for so much performance potential."

To correct this, Mr. McCahill said, the Edsel people were offering, *at additional cost,* something called an "export kit," consisting of heavier springs and shock absorbers. In other words, the company was flatly admitting its assembly-line car was incorrectly suspended, and if you wanted one that was correctly suspended, you'd have to pay extra for it. "For my dough," Mr. McCahill told *Mechanix Illustrated's* fascinated readers, "I wouldn't own one except with the export kit; without stiffer suspension, a car with so much performance could prove similar to opening a Christmas basket of King Cobras in a small room with the lights out."

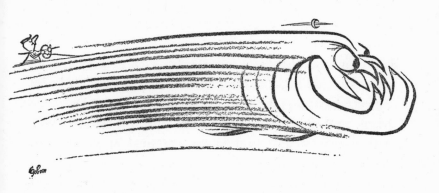

Mr. McCahill discovered the Edsel, despite its wildly spinning wheels, could achieve 60 miles an hour in 8.7 seconds from a standing start, and 30 miles and hour in three seconds from ground zero. Still, there was some small difficulty. "To do this," Mr. McCahill explained, "I was forced to feather the throttle to avoid wheel break and I couldn't help but wonder what this salami would really do if it had enough road adhesion to keep the wheels from spinning and you could shove the throttle through to the front axle."

Perhaps all this is not the fault it seems, however, because it might just be that cars should not instantly respond to the desires of people who want to jam throttles through the floorboards in an attempt to jump from nothing to 30 in *less* than three seconds. It would seem that the Edsel is already lethal enough, because let us suppose that a man is stopped at a traffic light. He is the kind of person who jams throttles to axles the split second a light changes.

There he is—let's call him Sneed—not looking at the red light facing him, but at the yellow caution light diagonally across the intersection. The instant that yellow light blinks, Sneed will leap ahead.

At the same moment, a school child starts to run across the street on what is left of the yellow light. The light blinks off. The child hesitates, starts to continue across the street, thinks better of it, and starts back to the curb. Meantime, Sneed, watching the yellow light to the exclusion of all else, has jammed his accelerator. Then, horrified, he sees the running child who is now pelting back toward safety. Sneed jams on the brake.

Unfortunately, Sneed's salami, as Mr. McCahill would call it, is already traveling across a yards-wide intersection at nearly 20 miles an hour, gaining speed and momentum every inch of the way. Under perfect traffic conditions, given normally-functioning brakes and a normal human reaction time, the average driver in the average car traveling at 25 miles an hour cannot possibly come to a halt in less than 44 feet from the spot where danger was first perceived.

Hence, in the instant it takes Sneed to see the child, realize his error, take his foot from accelerator and slam it on the brake, and for the brake then to take hold and begin to stop the wheels, and so cause the vast steel juggernaut to lose all momentum, the child is dead.

One wonders why.

What dream has Detroit fulfilled? What illusion made real?

To return to more humdrum matters, the basic tragedy of the Edsel's design was not that it was a hot car improperly suspended, nor that it was necessary to buy additional equipment to cure its little faults, but that it was not a *different* car. It was just another big, gaudy, not-too-unusual-looking entry in what is euphemistically called the middle price range, following established trends. For instance, in 1956, *Consumer Reports* summed up the new "1957" models as "lower, wider and longer, but having no more room inside; more power and, despite higher compression ratios, lapping up more and more super-fuel; more speed and hotter performance; a little better handling; more inadequately supported hardtop roofs, more glass area, increasingly wrapped-around windshields embodying more entrance difficulty and glass distortion; added weight not always reflected in stiffer structure; fatter and squealier tires that make parking harder without power steering and lastly, higher prices." In 1957, when the "1958" models appeared, *The New York Times* summed them up as follows: "They will cost more. They will have more horsepower. They will have improved engines, which may give more miles to a gallon of [more expensive] gas. They will cost more to repair. There will be more models . . . about the only thing there will not be more of is comfort, especially when the new six-passenger car has a full load." The Edsel was in this tradition.

105

The only reason to believe the Edsel was the particular car for the younger executive family on its way up was that the advertisements said so.

"Edsel specifications," *Consumer Reports* said in 1957, "reveal no major engineering advances and offer few mechanical —or functional—details that won't appear on Ford or Mercury for 1958."

The Ranger and Pacer models, *Consumer Reports* said, had the same components as Ford Fairlanes "including the Ford Fairlane's far-from-roomy body structure." Likewise, Corsairs and Citations were filled with Mercury components and the only thing *Consumer Reports* had to say about the new Edsel engines was that they "were going to have big appetites . . . but . . . they almost certainly will require super-premium fuel."

The Edsel, *Consumer Reports* said, "appears to be an unexciting automobile mechanically; durable, no doubt, probably longer lasting, probably better riding than the Ford, but in the main offering the Ford and Mercury virtues over again at slightly different prices. But Edsels are, indeed, very highly gadgeted . . . there are enough flashing lights on the instrument panel to satisfy pinball machine addicts.

"Merchandising advantage," the report concluded, "rather than the desire to create a really new, different or better automobile, seems to be the Edsel's reason for being."

Truer words were never cast in movable type.

The big question remaining is whether the Edsel achieved any merchandising advantage for Ford that the company could not better have achieved by bringing out a new kind of car. At this writing, the answer seems to be fairly clear.

The Edsel arrived in showrooms on September 4, 1957. By September 30, the nation's 1,160 new Edsel dealers had their first forebodings—people weren't buying. In fact, some were snickering. October sales were even lower than September's; November sales were lower than October's. By midwinter, some Edsel dealers were bankrupt—cleaned out in three months—and others were trying to get out from under as fast as they could. Desperately, Ford sank another ten million dollars into Edsel advertising, but so far this seems to have had no effect other than to prove you shouldn't throw good money after bad. There is every indication that the decision to manufacture the Edsel was one of the most costly blunders in all

merchandising history, and many an advertising man is beginning to take his own long, second look at the practitioners of motivation research and market analysis.

With the gift of hindsight, we can say yes, if Ford had introduced a really new car in the fall of 1957, its chances would have been better than the chances of the look-alike, act-alike models of "1958" Chrysler, Ford and General Motors products. It is equally easy to see that a genuinely new car will capture the market tomorrow because someone will someday have to reverse the current trends if for no other reason than the simple fact that cars cannot indefinitely grow longer, lower, wider, more powerful, more wasteful and more expensive. Also, if Detroit is going to market automobiles like dresses, Detroit will have to steel itself against flighty Dame Fashion's abrupt changes, and the first company really to do something radically sensible is going to corner the market.

At this point, I'll suggest that the possibility for a company to make a fortune existed at least since 1947, and that the only reason—apart from a lack of courage and a surfeit of blind greed—that nobody took advantage of it was that nobody in Detroit remembered, or cared about or understood Tom Wretch.

Tom is a member of that great middle majority that reaches from the upper-lower through the lower-middle class. In a word, he doesn't have much money and he's not too bright. Tom drives his car to work. He buys a car and drives it until it's worn out, and then he has it fixed and drives it a little longer, because he just can't afford a new one every year. Most often, he buys a used car. At the same time, Tom reads all

poor Wretch!

about the new models, and in his own good-natured way, he actually believes what he reads. He thinks cars *are* getting better and better, just as the advertisements say.

Tom is a little slow, but he's not entirely a dunce. He might be easy to mislead, but he is honest with himself, and he's not given to venting his aggressive impulses by endangering the life of every kid on the block at fifty miles an hour through a residential zone. He doesn't buy a car because it reminds him of his high school sweetheart's underwear, or because the car permits him to think he's General Patton. For example, he has a spotlight on his old General Chrysford coupé. He didn't buy it because of some hidden urge to pretend he was a fire chief. He bought it because he really uses it to find door numbers in strange neighborhoods. Likewise, that extra-long antenna doesn't reflect Tom's urge to attract attention. Tom bought it hoping it would (as advertised) improve his radio reception. (It didn't.) There is no doubt that Tom will buy any gadget he thinks he can use, if he has the money. Tom buys the cheapest model in the low price field because that's all he can afford if, indeed, he can really afford *that*. We're going to look in on him in 1953, when a marketing revolution was underway, and when the car that seemed to offer Tom the most for the least was a General Chrysford Stylepack Super. Tom liked everything about that car, including the price, which, like all automobile prices, was far beyond his means.

As we follow Tom Wretch through his little problems, remember this about him: Tom really wanted that Stylepack Super. If, however, there had been a less gadget-bedizened

110

contraption on the market, selling for $495—or nearly $2,200 less than Tom paid for his Stylepack—would Tom have taken it?

Our $495 figure doesn't come out of thin air, by the way. In his *Get a Horse,* Mr. M. M. Musselman reports that Detroit could have manufactured a light, practical machine for that price in 1950. And, in *My Forty Years With Ford* (Norton, N. Y., 1956) Charles E. Sorensen, the man who had as much to do with the Model T as Henry Ford, says a light, cheap car in the Model T tradition "is possible today, but only under certain conditions.

"One is a reversal of the present trend in auto design and in public preference," Mr. Sorensen writes. "Today's cars are more wasteful of power and fuel than any that have gone before. . . . For speed and power the American people are paying dearly, not only in safety but in unnecessarily inefficient operation and gas consumption. . . . The most economically operating cars today are the light, small, low horsepower ones of foreign make. They come from countries which tax horsepower instead of size or weight. . . . Even with import duties, some of them can be sold in the United States for less [than our cheapest cars]."

When Tom went into the market in 1953, there were no bargains, foreign or domestic, and Tom bought what he could. Now, just for the sake of argument, let's say that Tom had some depths to be probed, after all. Let's say he really would be pleased with a Cadillac; that he dreams futile dreams of wealth and satyriasis. It is obvious he cannot buy a Cadillac, but there are two cars he *can* buy—on time. They're both new.

111

Both are two-door sedans. One looks very much like a small version of the Cadillac that haunts Tom's subconscious mind. It costs $2,500. The other has only the Roman virtue of practicality and the Scottish virtue of thrift. It travels forty miles on a gallon of gasoline and it costs $500. Are Tom's dreams worth $2,000 to him?

Well, sir and lady, it's difficult to say. History can be confusing. There is no question the Model T lost its sales leadership to Chevrolet when the Chevrolet trended diffidently into dreamboat realms. In 1927, however, everybody might have wanted a car, but not every man could afford one—not even a Model T. Is it not more correct to read into the Model T's demise the presumption that any man who could buy a Model T could also find a way to buy something flashier, given the chance? And that now, when people like Tom Wretch are dependent on automobiles, those Wretches would buy a latter-day version of a Model T, given the chance?

Is not the real reason why Detroit builds dreamboats simply so that it can sell six million $2,500 cars on the installment plan, and thus make *five billion more dollars* than if it sold twenty million $500 cars? Is this not the real reason why there is no latter-day Model T on the road, no matter *what* the public wants? If Detroit thinks of Tom Wretch at all, does it not merely regard him as the kind of clod who will have to buy a *used* car—a purchase which has the virtue of keeping the whole zany scheme of automobile financing in something resembling balance?

As this is written, only two kinds of new automobiles are selling well in the American market. One is the foreign car

Mr. Sorensen describes, and the other is the American Motors' compromise, the Rambler. The Rambler is not as small as the foreign car, yet it is shorter than the smallest Detroit dreamboat. It is slightly more expensive than the foreign car; slightly less expensive than the cheapest Detroit make. It is cheaper to operate than the Detroit thing; a little more expensive than the foreign car. Do the sales of Ramblers and foreign cars portend a bright future for any manufacturer willing to gamble all on the success of a really new, really cheap, serviceable car? Will somebody discover Tom Wretch and make another Woolworth fortune?

I mention this *en passant* for what it might be worth: The Volkswagen people are so busy trying to fill their orders that they do not need the services of market analysts, researchers, psyche-plumbers, hidden persuaders and twenty million dollars' worth of advertising.

Meanwhile, let's now join Tom Wretch as he goes to market to fall victim to a pattern of merchandising first devised in a Levantine *souk*. Next, we'll find out what Wretch *really* bought, as compared with what he *thought* he bought when he delivered himself up to the usurers. When we've finished with Wretch, we might want to reflect again on the Edsel's history to see if it does not somehow remind us of a general hastening to be the fustest with the mostest, but arriving on the wrong battlefield—and two years late.

HEIGH HO, COME TO THE FAIR!

THERE WAS NO DOUBT Tom Wretch needed an automobile. His position as elevator captain at the Mausoleum Self-Service Products Corporation depended on his arriving punctually at 7:30 A.M. five days a week, and Tom lived in a housing development twenty miles from the heart of Metropolis. There was neither train nor bus, and nobody's car pool left the devolopment at six in the morning. There was, however, Tom's 1950 General Chrysford two-door coupé, and its doors were sprung, one window was broken, the valves leaked, the fenders were nearly rusted off, the muffler was shot, the wheel bearings were noisy, the gears didn't mesh until the third try, and the tires were threadbare. From time to time, Wretch thought about another car, by which he meant another used car, because his $75 salary seemed to set certain limits on his ambitions.

Tom's ambitions, however, were as unimportant as his capabilities, because while he was considering his automotive needs, forces quite beyond his control were conspiring to give him not a new used car, but a brand-new car. It is an irony of our time that the same forces entirely depended on Tom's existence for their own, as we shall see. Meanwhile, Wretch finally said to himself, "I'll buy a car" one Saturday morning in 1953, not knowing that he would actually do so before the day was out. It was Simon Greed who made up Tom's mind for him. Mr. Greed had been laboring mightily all the week before to do just that, not quite without Tom's being aware of it.

Mr. Greed, president, general manager and sales director of Honor Bright Motors, Inc., was essentially a simple man. He simply wanted to sell more automobiles, and all of his considerable energies were concentrated on his problem. At last, one night, while he was nibbling his wife's ear, a great light flooded his mind. He would stage what the auto industry was first to call the "blitz," and then to come to know as a way of life.

At this point, permit me a slight digression. I have chosen to send Tom Wretch to Mr. Greed's market in 1953, because —according to testimony before the United States Senate— 1953 was the year the blitz first appeared in finest flower, and because the Senate has been kind enough to document the case. All of Mr. Greed's curious business practices (as well as a complete account of his troubles) will be found in "Automobile Marketing Practices," a 1,225-page typescript of hearings before the Senate's subcommittee of the Interstate and

115

Foreign Commerce Committee, eighty-fourth Congress, second session, published as Document 73438 by the U.S. Government Printing Office at Washington, D.C., in 1956. As we follow Tom Wretch through his purchase of an automobile, please bear in mind the fact that nothing has been made up. Senate testimony, according to the Senate's published document, indicates that my mythical Mr. Greed merely followed in detail the sales advice furnished him by at least one major manufacturer. Not all dealers are Simon Greed, of course—but Simon Greed is the sum of all dealers as described by themselves and other witnesses before the Senate. On this thought, let's now look in on Mr. Greed as, his sales force assembled about him, he waited for an abject silence, and then said huskily into this silence:

"Fellows, we're going to make history. Fellows, Honor Bright's going to sell one hundred brannew Stylepack Supers in one single, solitary day."

The salesmen stirred suspiciously. Honor Bright normally sold fewer than 400 cars in an entire year. Mr. Greed, however, was well aware that most historical events require a certain amount of mundane preparation, and he therefore let his troops in on the practical details.

First, he said, there would be extensive local radio, television and newspaper advertising, climaxed by a parade of one hundred new Stylepack Supers led down Main Street by a marching band. Pretty girls from Metropolis High would ride in the cars, and airplanes would soar overhead, towing signs reading HONOR BRIGHT.

Two cashiers would be hired for the day, Mr. Greed said,

and hot lunch would be served to the salesmen at their desks in order to create in the customers' minds the idea that Honor Bright was so busy selling cars that its salesmen didn't have time to go out for lunch. A cameraman would be on hand with a Polaroid camera to take a picture of salesman and customer every time a sale was consummated, and the lucky customer would be given the picture as a souvenir. Meanwhile, a band would play "music suitable to this occasion," as Mr. Greed put it, and all the while girls would serve free coffee to salesmen and customers alike.

"Fellows," Mr. Greed said, "it's going to be a *great* day. I'm going to give every man in this organization five silver dollars every time I see him being extra polite to a customer, and I'm going to give it to him right on the spot so the customer can see the value we put on courtesy.

"We're going to start selling at nine A.M. on Saturday morning and we're going to sell right through the night—oh, sure, there'll be searchlights and the band will be playing and you'll have food right along, and we're going to keep selling until nine A.M. Sunday morning when the customers can knock off and go to church. And we're going to sell a hundred cars in that day.

"Gentlemen," Mr. Greed said, drawing himself to attention, "I salute you."

Whereupon, he saluted them.

Next, Mr. Greed told his army that he wanted every man on the telephone all week before the sale, but not to make calls on the quarter hours, when Honor Bright's commercials would be running on radio and television. He drew diagrams, he outlined sales talks, but above all, Simon Greed gave his infantry a cause for which to fight. The cause was Service, because Mr. Greed was a public-spirited citizen. In his office there was a sign that ever reminded him, "Boost, don't knock." Wholly apart from his perfectly normal desire to make money, Simon Greed honestly wanted more people to own new cars, because he thought it was good for them, good for Metropolis, and good for him. He often said as much at Rotary revels. "What's good for Greed is good for Metropolis," he'd say.

Thus, it is only fair to say the whole idea of Mr. Greed's blitzkrieg was to help other people. Mr. Greed had asked himself this question: "Who needs help the most?" His answer was automatic. It was, "The people who can't afford a new car." Mr. Greed's problem was therefore clear. It was to find a way to sell new cars to people who couldn't afford them. Mr. Greed had found the way, and his solution was staggering in its awesome simplicity, and when he realized that the less able a man was to buy a car, the more money

119

that he, Greed, would make, the better this made Mr. Greed feel. He experienced that soaring of the soul that had led Mr. Henry Ford to his tremendous dictum: "We know now that anything which is economically right is also morally right."

Here, briefly, was Mr. Greed's idea:

Only one kind of customer was to be kept out of the shop. That was the man who wanted to pay cash. A man like that, Mr. Greed figured, didn't need help.

"On a sale like this, cash customers can kill you," Mr. Greed said. "We're practically giving the car away as it is. So if a guy hauls out a checkbook and says 'how much?' you write the order and send for me. I'll explain to the guy that Gee, we've been selling so fast the salesmen don't know we don't have a car left in stock, and all we can do now is take orders. I'll tell him we'll be glad to take his order, but it might take him a couple of months to get the car, and meanwhile, can we show him the convertible."

Cash customers were a remote danger, however, and it was for the overwhelming bulk of his clientele that Mr. Greed had two prices in mind. The first, to be charged relatively solvent customers, would guarantee Honor Bright a barest minimum profit of more than $12,000 if all 100 cars were sold. The second price was more of an elastic plan than it was a price, and there was no possible way of reckoning the day's profits in advance, except to say that $12,000 would be chicken feed if all 100 cars were sold according to the plan.

Since Mr. Greed's sale did make history indeed, and became not only the rage of 1953, but was recommended as a model by one giant manufacturer, and reached gaudy heights in 1955, and has remained the vogue to date, it is instructive to follow Mr. Greed's arithmetic in some detail.

First, Mr. Greed knew the factory would charge him $1,726.97 for a Stylepack Super loaded with radio, heater, overdrive, white sidewall tires, and other odds and ends. He figured he could give a $30 commission to his salesman (above salary), spend—or at least, charge—$15 to have the car put into running order (this is called the handling charge, of which more later), tack on a $39.38 gross profit, and offer the car to a "solvent" customer for $1,811.35. (Of course, Mr. Greed could have put a stripped-down car on sale for $354.97 less, but he wanted his customers to have the very best. He thought they not only deserved it, but would want nothing less.)

If Mr. Greed's "solvent" customer provided either $454 in cash, or turned in a used car worth that much, this would leave the customer owing an unpaid balance of $1,357.35. Mr. Greed would then add in $144.50 for thirty months of insurance, leaving the purchaser to finance a balance of $1,501.85, on which there would be 6% interest for thirty months. This was not interest on a declining balance, however —it was more in the nature of a carrying charge—and thus the customer would be faced with a total of $1,772.18 to be divided into monthly payments. In other words, the customer would first have to pay $454 down in one shape or another, and then $1,772.18 in monthly payments, or—to be blunt about it—it would cost the customer a grand total of $2,226.18 to buy a car that cost Simon Greed exactly $1,771.97 to sell.

It must not be imagined that Mr. Greed would make anything like a $454.21 profit on each deal, however. His gross profit was $39.38 on the car, plus an $82.97 profit on the

121

finance and insurance charges. Thus, Mr. Greed himself would make only $122.35 on each deal, but then, he was simply out for volume, as he said. If he sold 100 cars in one day on these terms, his profits would be $12,235 for the day, and he could expect his profits on the finance charges of his used-car sales to more than wash out the cost of advertising his new-car blitz.

It will be seen that Mr. Greed's profit on finance charges was more than twice the gross profit on the sale of the car itself. If, like many other dealers, Mr. Greed's profits on parts and service had paid for the entire overhead of his sales agency, and if Mr. Greed had further owned his finance company, Mr. Greed's profits would tell a much longer and more interesting story. Alas, this was not the case. Mr. Greed, like many more dealers then and now, earned only .8% net profit on sales of new and used cars, parts and service, and his real profit was made on financing and acting as an agent for an insurance company. It is precisely this point that gave rise to the truly monumental phase of Mr. Greed's blitz—the plan for the customers who couldn't afford to buy. The plan for people like Tom Wretch.

For one solid week, Wretch could not look up on his way home from work without seeing Mr Greed's airplanes. He could not turn on his radio or television set or read any page of the Metropolis *Morning & Sunday Patriot* without being somehow aware of Honor Bright's story. On Saturday morning, the story appeared on the *Patriot's* centerfold in 64-, 36- and 24-point type:

IT'S WHEEL AND DEAL AT HONOR BRIGHT!

Never before, and never again, will we be trading as high, wild, handsome and zany!

WE'LL POSITIVELY TOP ANY DEAL IN TOWN!

Yes, folks, even if your car has to be *towed* to our lot, we may give you at least $800 for it! Up to $1,500 on your 1950 car! But that's not all!

WHEN YOU BUY TODAY, WE'LL GIVE YOU $300 IN CASH, TO BE USED FOR ANY PURPOSE!

No, folks, this isn't part of your trade-in! It's a bonus from us to you!

WE CAN DO THIS BECAUSE WE'RE GOING TO SELL 100 BRAND NEW STYLEPACK SUPERS IN *ONE DAY!*

Yes, folks, 100 cars must go even if we have to give 'em away! Trade-ins? WE DON'T CARE! Down payments! WE DON'T CARE! Terms? WE DON'T CARE! Profits! WE DON'T CARE! WE WANT VOLUME!

Yes, folks, Honor Bright is going volume crazy! And here's why! We want people to have the best car made! We know, and you know, the bigger the volume, the more you can cut profits, and the more you cut profits the more friends you make! So come on out to Honor Bright today, have a free lunch on us, tell us your terms, and don't feel obliged to buy! Of course, you'll want to buy when you see the new Stylepack Super and find out that we'll meet any terms you set!

WE'LL MAKE DEALS WITH NOTHING DOWN!
to properly qualified customers

The advertisement was tastefully embellished with photographs of girls kissing young men who were buying them Stylepack Supers. The automobiles were strangely long and low, because Mr. Greed used the manufacturer's press-release photographs in which, by clever distortion, the center section of each car is increased by one-third, and the girls and young men stand on boxes well in the foreground to make the cars seem even lower. It was another magnificent illustration of the fact that the camera does more than writers can to justify Detroit to man.

Wretch, whose unconscious ear had been bombared all week by Mr. Greed's drumfire; Wretch, weakened by his obvious need for another car, was nevertheless still somewhat suspicious of what seemed too good a thing to be true, but Henry Clapperclaw finally disarmed him. Mr. Clapperclaw, city editor of the *Patriot,* privately was given to understand there just might be a special deal at Honor Bright for him, particularly if Mr. Clapperclaw's sense of news judgment led Mr. Clapperclaw to want to run a little something of his own, in the news sections of the paper, concerning Honor Bright's one-day philanthropy. Like many city editors, Mr. Clapperclaw was something of a junior-grade back-scratcher, and in order that Honor Bright should not be uninformed as to who were Honor Bright's friends, Mr. Clapperclaw modestly signed his name and title to the page one story that Tom Wretch read. And reading, Wretch concluded that if the paper said so, it must be true. Wherefore, Wretch roused himself, put on hat and coat, and rummaged for his car keys.

"Where you goin', hon?" Mae Wretch asked.

"Out," Tom explained. "Be back soon."

Wretch smiled to himself. That'd make Mae mad, not knowing where he was going, he thought, but she'd be tickled silly when she saw the surprise he'd bring home. He was still smiling to himself when Honor Bright's doors were flung open to give him entrance.

"Hello, sir, we're *real* glad *you* came to see us today," Bob Joy boomed, pumping Wretch's hand and grasping him by the sleeve. "It's sure good of *you* to drop by, but then, heh, we know why you're here."

Wretch, barely past the doorjamb, looked a bit at sea. Five men had converged on him, but this one had caught him and was leading him to a desk. Bob Joy was Simon Greed's star salesman.

"Siddown," Joy said generously. "Have a cup coffee? Here, let me light that *for* you."

He snapped a silver lighter before Wretch's cigarette.

"*You* don't really want to *see* the new Stylepack Super, do you?" Joy rattled on, before Wretch could say a word. "I can see *you* know just as well as we know that it's the best thing anybody ever put on the road. You look to me like the kind of man that *really knows cars*—the kind that reads the specifications before he ever comes to the shop. Right?"

"Well, sure I read about—" Wretch began.

"Right!" Joy said. "So the only thing *you* want to know is style, color, how soon you can have it, and the terms. Right?"

"Ah," Wretch said.

"Right!" Joy said. "How soon can you have it? Ten minutes from now. Style? It's the Stylepack Super, fully equipped, the hottest thing in the whole General Chrysford family, the car that wowed 'em at the auto show. Color? Most of 'em here on the lot today are the new tri-colors—bile green, jararaca red, and prune-pit puce. I mean, they're the same crisp tricolors that took the auto show big. So I guess that's what you'd want anyway. But if it isn't, well, we have others to choose from. So let's not worry about color."

"Could I—" Wretch said. "I just came to look around . . . I . . . well, I have a car. Outside. I mean, I don't know what kind of . . ."

"What kind of deal you want to make?" Joy grinned. "Tell you what—let's see your car."

He jumped around the desk, swept Wretch from his chair, pushed Honor Bright's door open, and hustled Wretch outside. There, across the street from the glittering Stylepacks, was Tom's 1950 coupé with its eroded fenders.

"Glad to see you have one of our General Chrysford family," Joy said. "Plenty of life in this baby. You took good care of it, didn't you?"

"Well, yes, kind of," Wretch agreed.

"I believe you," Joy said. Then, doing some quick arithmetic in the tumblers of his mind, Joy thought to himself that Wretch's wreck would bring $400 at most at auction after the tiny rust holes in the fenders were filled with wax and lampblack. Joy felt he could sell it to a customer for more, of course, but $400 would have to be a basing price. That was $54 less than Wretch would need as a downpayment on Simon Greed's $1,811 price schedule. Obviously, Wretch wouldn't have $54 in his pockets, much less in a bank. But Wretch might be good for sixty a month. So, Joy thought, I'll slip him the pack. . . .

"Tell you what, friend," Joy said, "I'll give you seven hundred for that car of yours, and that's what I'd call a deal, hey?"

"But this is a 1950 job," Wretch said. "Your ad said you'd give fifteen hundred on a 1950 car, and eight hundred even if it had to be towed to the lot."

"I don't think it said *that*," Joy smiled. "It said we *may* give you eight hundred on a car you have to tow to the lot. Like, if you had a new Rolls-Royce and the battery was dead, so you had to tow it in, we might go up to eight hundred on it, and like, if your '50 was a fully equipped convertible with only ten miles on it, we'd maybe go up to near one thousand five hundred.

"But I tell you true," Joy said seriously, "seven hundred is a top price for your car, because we couldn't sell it for that. Not with these new Stylepacks out now, that everybody wants. But, if you think you can get a better deal, why that's all right with us.

"Besides," he confided, "if you make the deal, we'll take your car as the down payment, so there'll be nothing down to you, nothing at all, and—on top of that, if you buy today we'll give you $300 in cash to use for any purpose.

"Now, nobody's got a deal like that," he said. "This way, we're really giving you $1000 for your old car, aren't we? But don't tell."

There was something infectious about Joy's grin, and so, Wretch smiled at Joy.

"Come on in," Joy said, "have a cup coffee while we figure it out. . . ."

The whole key to Simon Greed's blitz lay in the fact that nowhere in his advertising, nowhere in his shop, did Greed once mention the "list price" of his wares. The actual price to be quoted by salesmen was left to that salesman's discretion, as long as it did not go below the $1,811 figure that was the basic "list price" to solvent customers. Following Mr. Greed's formula for selling to people like Wretch, Bob Joy raced through a series of transpositions. First, as noticed, he had inflated the worth of Wretch's old wreck by $300. Next, he added $300 to the original $1,811.35 that was the basic "list price" of the day's sale, to quote Wretch the figure of $2,111.35 as the "list price" of the Stylepack Super. The mythical $300 was what Joy called the "pack."

Joy thereupon deducted $700 allowed on Wretch's car as the down payment, on the theory that $700 was one-third of $2,100, and that any 36-month term contract should carry at least a third down.*

This left an unpaid balance of $1411.35, to which Joy quickly added $144.50 for insurance, and then added the "$300 cash gift" to bring the unpaid balance to finance up to $1,855.85. Next, figuring three years at 6% on all this, he added in $334.05 to bring the total for Wretch to finance up to an imposing $2,189.90, which he expressed in these terms:

"So it's only $60.83 a month to you."

---

* Four hundred dollars, you see, was not one-third of $1,800, but $700 was one-third of $2,100. The reader will object that neither is $454 one-third of $1811.35, but mysterious are the ways of auto finance. Greed arrived at his $454 figure on the basis of $1,362, which is what a stripped Stylepack cost him. He did not count the $354.97 worth of optional equipment in making his down-payment estimate.

Thus, Wretch would be paying out $2,589.90 in notes and investment to buy the car that cost Mr. Greed precisely $1,771.97 to sell, or, to put it another way, it would cost Wretch exactly $363.72 more to buy the same car than it would cost anyone able to meet Mr. Greed's "solvent customer" price on a thirty-month deal.

Wretch would now be paying a 6% "interest" on a balance that never declined; he would be paying it on $300 that turned out not to be a gift, but a loan; he would be paying 6% on a $300 "pack" that was pure whimsy; he would be paying 6% on Mr. Greed's insurance commission; he would be paying state sales and personal property taxes on a base of $2,189.90 when his purchase was really worth $1,771.97, so that he would also be paying taxes on the very interest he paid. We might redundantly reflect that Wretch would be paying more taxes on his purchase than a rich man who paid cash would pay on the same purchase.

In sum, Wretch would be paying a total of $478.10 in charges on a $2,100 deal, and since Simon Greed made a 20% profit on gross charges, this meant that Greed would make a $95.62 profit on this amount, plus his $39.38 gross profit on the sale of the car itself, or a total of $135 profit on a sale to Wretch. Thus, Mr. Greed would earn $13.65 more per car by selling to people like Wretch than he would by selling to anyone who met his other price. In this way did Mr. Greed work his wonders to perform; in this way did he help those who seemed least able to help themselves; in this way did Mr. Greed do his bit to help make Metropolis great. No knocker, but a booster, he.

But how was Wretch going to be able to pay $60.83 a

month for a new car when his salary was only $75 a week? When he also had a mortgage to pay and a wife and three children to feed? In view of Wretch's financial structure, why didn't he buy a secondhand bicycle instead?

Curiously enough, these questions are easy to answer. Like most Americans, Tom Wretch thought of the automobile as a means of transportation, indeed, as the only means of transportation, and then at once dismissed the thought. Like most Americans, Tom Wretch thought of the automobile as more than that. To him, the automobile was really not so much a means of transportation as it was a state of mind. It must be understood that Tom Wretch *really wanted* that Stylepack Super. Not only did he want a Stylepack, but he also really wanted all those optional doodads with which Mr. Greed had thoughtfully festooned it. Mr. Greed's estimate of Mr. Wretch's desires was exact. More—much more—will be said on this point; please note it now and have MacArthur's faith that we shall return.

The next thing to understand is that Wretch signed on hope —on the hope that tomorrow will be just as good as today, and probably better. Further, he thought he was getting a whale of a deal, getting $1,000 for his old car. He did not believe the thief in himself was, in fact, the victim. To Tom Wretch, the fact was this: he'd drive home with a new Stylepack, kiss his wife at the door, and hand her $300 in cash. If a pinch should come in the days ahead, we may be sure Wretch could gladly pinch himself, because as sociologists Robert and Helen Lynd pointed out in their *Middletown*, people earning as little as $35 a week reported "We'd rather do without clothes than give up the car . . . I'd go without food before I see us give up the car." In the midst of the Depression, the Lynds found the family car the one depression-proof commodity—everything else was more vulnerable. Marriages, new babies, clothing and food disappeared from the American scheme of values while the automobile remained. There was no depression in 1953, of course, but in the intervening twenty years since the Lynds' report the automobile had become even more important in the American scheme of things. Who has not seen the Cadillac parked before the hovel? The government estimates that two million Americans who earn less than $750 a year somehow own cars. So naturally, Wretch signed up; gladly he drove home with his debt.

Wretch's attitude is significant; it made Simon Greed's blitz possible. Yet, Mr. Greed's blitz is significant too, because it started a nationwide trend that, in retrospect, leads us to envision Robert Joy as Galahad and Simon Greed as sweetly pure as Candide.

Joy's "pack" quickly became known to an expanding trade as the "top pack," which can take the form either of a purely fictitious list price, or an inflated turn-in price on a used car with the same price added to the new car purchase price. In addition, there emerged, and there is the "plain pack"—a purely mythical amount of money charged for various mysterious services which either do not exist, or are not performed, or, if performed, actually cost much less.

Then there is the "finance pack," whereby dealers more than make up in finance charges for any gross profits that might be squeezed out of a sale by low "list prices." Using rate charts furnished by finance companies, dealers can set their rates so high that they can sell the contract to a finance agency at a discount and still receive an extra profit for themselves. Overcharges on insurance provide a rich vein of ore, and when finance and insurance charges are added together and then presented to the customer in the form of "here's your monthly payment"—which, despite the Federal Trade Commission's orders governing itemized bills of sale, is often done—then the customer has no way of knowing what in the world he is paying to whom, or why.

There is the "switch." This simply consists of advertising a genuine bargain, and then telling customers it's been sold, switching their attention to quite another deal.

What automobile dealers call "the bush," or "bushing," means offering a bargain, then hiking the price during the course of the sale. A salesman may actually quote one price, get a customer to sign a blank sales agreement, and then, when all is signed, write in a much higher price than he quoted. Or, he may write his quoted price on the sales agreement, have the customer sign the document, and then say, "I'll have to get the manager's approval."

Instants later, he's back with an irate manager at his heels.

"My God, the kind of salesmen we get these days," the manager apologizes to the customer. "One more mistake like that and I'll have to fire him. Look, friend, he gave you the wrong price. The real price is $2,597, not $2,465, and even then I'm giving it away with no profit at all, just because of my man's mistake."

Then, while the chastised salesman cringes in the background, the manager concludes the sale to which the customer is already emotionally committed, but at the higher price. "Bushing" is so profitable it has deprived Broadway of some major talent.

Then, there is the "highball." There is also the "low ball." To highball, a salesman verbally offers a customer a high price on a trade-in while they're outside the shop, and then offers much less when the customer has picked out and is about to sign for a new car. When a salesman throws a low ball, he either "bushes" or gives the customer less for his used car than it is worth, or both.

"Would You Take" is a simple highball. A card is tucked under a windshield wiper on your parked car. The card says "would you take $10,000,000 for this dog as a trade-in on a new Jetzoom?" Sure, you'd take it. But when you get to the store, you're bushed, highballed, lowballed, packed plain, top-packed, finance packed, or, possibly, "unhorsed."

Of all the sales practices in vogue, unhorsing is perhaps the ultimate refinement. "This is a rising market in used cars," the salesman says. "Tell you what. You give us your car. We'll lend you a new car. By next month, we'll get you $500 more for your used car than you can get now, and then we'll sell it and close the deal on the new car. Your new-car guarantee starts when you actually buy it next month. What could be fairer than that?"

Nothing would be more fair if that happy chain of circumstances should, by chance, be forged. But at the end of the month, the salesman says, "Gee, Mac, we sold your old lemon. But all we could get for it was $600 less than we thought we'd get, because the market went down instead of up. So now you don't have a car, but here's the dough. Now, are you gonna buy that new car, or not? If you don't, we'll have to charge you rent on all the time you've been driving it."

Finally, for the man who really can't afford to buy a bag of popcorn on time, there is the "balloon." A deal is worked out—no down payment, other than the used car or perhaps a judgment note or chattel mortgage against everything you own. There are as many as forty-eight months to pay, and the payments are fantastically low. All except the last one. Heretofore, the payments have been almost pure "interest," which is to say, the carrying charge, but the last payment is so large that the whole note must be refinanced, at, naturally, "interest" again.

We remarked that Mr. Greed's blitz occurred in 1953, but all of his sales practices have been in use since the first days of the automobile, or, perhaps, since the invention of the wheel. Greed's contribution was to use every gimmick all at once in a blitz—he was original only in the sense that Carlyle's most original man was he who adapts from the greatest number of sources. The important thing to understand about Mr. Greed's operation is that his combined attack—his military phrases, his girls, his Polaroid camera, his music, his parade, his searchlights, hot lunch, free coffee, 100-car day and so on—was recommended as an ideal by the Ford Motor Company in the pages of the September 10, 1953, issue of Ford's *Car Merchandising Bulletin,* published by Ford's Car Sales Department. Indeed, the Ford company seemed so happy with blitz operations that witnesses were to complain to the United States Senate that Ford deliberately set up company-owned dealerships to use blitz methods in competition with more reliable, established Ford dealers, in an effort to jazz up sales.

Similarly, Mr. Greed's misleading advertising, quoted above, is simply a combination of newspaper advertising bought by dealers. Such advertising has been repudiated by the manufacturers, but still, we note that it appears in nearly every big city newspaper nearly every day.

As for the sundry packs and the questionable, if not usurious trade practices, it should be clearly understood that no automobile manufacturer approves of them. Senate testimony indicated that manufacturers' sales division managers were firmly telling the dealers something like this: "We don't like the pack. All we want you to do is sell cars or lose your franchise. If the other guy down the street is using the pack, you may have to think about this. Remember, we don't like packs. All we want you to do is sell cars, make your quotas, or lose your franchise. So suit yourselves."

Nevertheless, it must be said that one witness told the Senate that, in 1955, General Motors Acceptance Corporation, General Motors' favorite finance company, practiced a singular duplicity. The witness, a former GM dealer, said "GMAC has two charts. If the dealer wants more kickbacks, they give him a high-priced chart."

Other former GM dealers were to testify that honorable sales practices which had prevailed during the pre-World War II regime of Alfred P. Sloan, Jr., as company president seemed to have been tossed overboard after Harlow Curtice took command of the giant corporation.

Indeed, the testimony moved Sen. Monroney to suggest that

135

"the renaissance of responsibility [and] ethical leadership enunciated by Mr. Sloan" had "gone into the limbo of forgotten words in Detroit."

Rather than connect Mr. Curtice with this state of things, we should recall Mr. Greed, and we should remember Mr. Wretch. It was Mr. Greed's knowledge of Mr. Wretch's business naïveté that made Mr. Greed's blitz possible, and Mr. Wretch's willingness to be blitzed that kept the thing going, and all this captured the imaginations of the division sales managers of the corporations. The division sales managers fed the blitz, and it spread like crab grass in 1953. By the end of 1955, the blitz had thrown the automobile retail market into such turmoil that Senator A. S. Mike Monroney (D., Oklahoma) remarked that the business of selling automobiles had taken on all "the morality of an Oriental bazaar."

Between January and March, 1956, Senator Monroney presided over a Senate hearing requested by—of all people—the automobile dealers. It seemed they wanted Congress to protect them from the manufacturers, from the public, and from themselves. As Senator Monroney remarked, it was astonishing to find the dealers asking Congress for legislation, because automobile dealers as a class generally tend to have as little use for what they call "government interference" as anyone to the distant right of the late Colonel Robert McCormick.

Meanwhile, blitzing had reached such proportions that a noise level seldom equaled by P. T. Barnum's pitchmen pervaded the bazaar. From New York to Portland new cars were being offered for "10¢ down, 10¢ a day," or for "sale at a 1¢ profit." A Cleveland dealer offered two new cars for $2,999.

Another Cleveland dealer offered 500 gallons of free gas with a new car purchase; the offer was doubled in Providence, Rhode Island. Detroit Chevrolet dealer Saul Rose said he'd give a customer a sleeping bag, a hammer, an ax, boots, a compass, a Geiger counter, maps of likely terrain, and, in event of his customer's failing to count any Geigers, he'd give the disappointed prospector 100 shares of somebody's uranium stock. Another Detroit dealer said he'd take a dollar off the price of a new Plymouth for every pound the customer and his wife weighed, or $1.50 off per pound on a Chrysler deal. In Denver and Portland, Oregon, customers were wooed with visions of trips to Hawaii; Bostonian purchasers were given a choice of Florida or Hollywood. Cleveland Pontiac purchasers were lured by a trip for two to Bermuda; uranium stock was offered in Birmingham; Alcoa stock in Marysville, Tennessee; General Motors stock came with a new car purchase in Miami and one dealer said he'd toss in three free shares of Ford stock to every man who bought a '56 Mercury. In Los Angeles—well, in Los Angeles all this sort of thing had never been particularly unusual, since as Frank Lloyd Wright points out, all our unstable elements seem to collect in lower California. In Los Angeles, smoky home of seven million automobiles, Senator Monroney's "Oriental bazaar" was a Hollywood production of an Oriental bazaar.

From one end of the nation to the other, dealers were buttonholing drivers at stoplights; fast-talking men in "boiler rooms" whirled telephone dials all day, running through the phone books. The "wheel and deal" was in full swing, and, let us note, the dealers were not alone. The manufacturers were adding their not-inconsequential weight to the fun. American Motors and Studebaker-Packard were offering free life insurance policies covering the buyer of a new car and his wife for the first year of their ownership. Dodge and Plymouth dealers were branch offices of a national lottery free to all—get an entry blank at your local dealer, fill it out, no obligation at all, and you just might win a new Dodge for every year of your life, or maybe, you would win $500 a month forever.

Advertising became more and more expert. Some advertisements turned out to be combinations of one car's price, another's picture, and the name of a third. At the same time, the "bootlegger" put in his appearance.

An automobile bootlegger, also called a "supermarket operator," does not sell a hot car. He buys cars from overstocked, but franchised dealers, paying slightly more than the dealer's wholesale price, but selling below the franchised dealer's "list price." Sometimes he sells his cars as "used—200 miles." Sometimes he sells them as "new used cars"; sometimes as "new." Most often, he will not say they are brand-new, all hot and crunchy off the assembly line, but he will say they are "1958 cars." He provides no parts, no service, and usually, no warranty. If he provides a new-car guarantee, he says you must go to a franchised dealer for your checks, services and repairs. Typically, he's just a lonely man with a neon sign and a vacant lot on the edge of town, and all he sells is cars, and he sells them with what Senator Monroney calls "a soldier's farewell." Cars come to him from a variety of sources, and one of the more popular is the Detroit dealer. Often, the cars are driven hundreds, if not thousands of miles from De-

troit to the bootlegger, chained together in pairs, their speedometers disconnected. If the trip is a long one, the original
"breaking in" oil is drained before the trip starts, and is re-
placed with regular oil. Or, oftener still, the cars are driven
to the bootlegger by some wayward adolescent, their break-
ing-in oil still in the crankcase. In either event, the result is
the same; the motor is more broken than in.

And, speaking of results, one result of all the hoopla in the
bazaar was that somebody, surely somebody, would eventually
have to pay for all the advertising, for all the free trips, for all
the free stock, for all the free gasoline, for all the national lot-
teries. Somebody owed a large bill for all the razzmatazz, not
to mention also owning a large bill for all those automobiles.
It was perhaps inevitable that the customer—Richard Rich
or Tom Wretch—should have to pick up the tab. Therefore,
the net worth of General Motors dealerships, for example,
climbed from 249 million dollars in 1940 to 2,200 million
dollars in 1956, and the profit on 17,000 GM dealerships for
the first nine months of 1955 alone was $414,000,000. It was
completely incomprehensible to Harlow Curtice that his, and
other dealers, seemed to be quite raddled with fear at this moment of their greatest prosperity.

Despite the blizzard of inflated dollars that drifted against
their doors, the dealers were a hag-ridden lot. They didn't
know how much of their net worth was real worth, and how
much was pure pack. They told Senator Monroney's committee they were forced by the manufacturers to do things that
were in the dealers' opinions unwise if not plain dishonest.

"When this thing became a shell game instead of a business," one former dealer said, he quit, "so I could live with myself."

Dealers said the manufacturers were locked in battle to see who could sell the most cars. General Motors, they said, was kneeing in the groin to maintain Chevrolet's sales lead over Ford; Ford was gouging and biting in the clinches to capture the lead from Chevrolet. This, in turn, compelled other manufacturers to bite, knee and scratch, too, if they were to compete at all with the giants. The dealers' position was peculiar. The manufacturer sells only to dealers; thus the manufacturers were really trying to see who could sell the most automobiles to dealers. Of course, the dealers would have to sell to somebody else, and if the manufacturers increased their volume to dealers, the dealers must do a greater volume of business with the public. If the dealers didn't reach the volume the manufacturer expected them to reach, the dealers would lose their franchises to sell the manufacturers' product.

So if we don't blitz, the dealers said, we lose our franchises. It was the manufacturers who told them to pack, some dealers said. The manufacturers had overproduced, and were cramming unwanted cars on the dealers, and then telling the dealers what subterfuges to employ to unload the junk on the public. At the same time, the dealers told the Senate, some manufacturers forced them to pay cash for cars when ordered, not when delivered, and this tied up so much of their working capital that they were strapped. One former dealer said he was shipped—and charged for—cars he had never ordered and had said he did not want.

Listening to an automobile dealer whine about his cruel

fate would ordinarily send a reasonable man into gales of laughter, but when the whines are extended over hundreds of pages of testimony, they take on a certain shy poignance, not without charm. One dealer said his manufacturer told him to set aside a certain quota of his cars for sale to a bootlegger; in other words, to set apart a certain amount of poison and then swallow it, for how can a franchised dealer sell cars at one price when the bootlegger sells them at a lower price? One dealer said he could get no new cars from his manufacturer while a bootlegger down the street had no trouble getting seventeen of them.

A Buick dealer said his manufacturer criticized him for not finding enough things wrong with cars brought to him for service. His sale of parts, it seemed, was too small. Another witness said sales division chiefs of Ford and General Motors requested dealers falsely to register cars in the names of their relatives and employees, to help win the sales race. A Chicago dealer said his sales boss told him he could bootleg his cars to Texas, for all the company cared, just as long as all the cars were registered as sold in Cook County, Illinois. The whines went on and on, and the clear burden of the song was that the manufacturers had put the dealers in great pain, and that it was the sales managers that were the villains of the piece. Dealers, Senator Monroney said, "show you letters from sales managers that you wouldn't write to a dog. . . . They [sales managers] have gone so far in some states as to require the dealer to violate the law. . . ."

The testimony was, that under pressure to sell and sell, the dealers adopted the pack as a way of life. Since the pack must surely come out of the car's price at some point on its road to the junk heap, this meant a simply incredible amount of dollars did not exist anywhere but on paper. In other words, many a customer owed more money on his car than that car was worth; thus the loan was unsecured. Some dealers said they had their names on the back of as much as $500,000 worth of paper, and that they frankly didn't know, and couldn't know whether this meant they were rich or bankrupt. On a 36-month sales contract, they said, eighteen months was the break-even point. For the first eighteen months, nothing was supporting the loan.

Dealers said they feared the 36- and 48-month terms on 1955 contracts would mean that 1955 buyers would be out of the market for the next three years, and they saw bleak days ahead. In this, of course, they were dead right. Dealers today tell you they haven't seen a profit for the last three years, but their wail leaves the public eye singularly dry. The public only too well remembers the bastinado it absorbed from the dealers in 1946–9, when the dealers had too few cars to sell, and sold them mercilessly. The public remembers (how can it forget, when a large part of it is still paying) the pack of 1955, when the dealers had too many cars to sell, and sold them mercilessly.

Senator Monroney, a patient man, listened to all the testimony, and it left him muttering darkly about "the juvenile delinquency that we are finding all over the country in the automobile business."

The shaky financial structure of the thing worried the Senator, and he summed up the dealer's position thus:

"You sell all the good credit risks, then the intermediate credit risks, then the ordinarily bad credit risks, and finally you get down to a guy who you don't know whether is going to wind up in Mexico in two weeks or not. But you sell him, with three years to pay."

Yes, the dealers nodded, that is so. But, they said, it's all the fault of the manufacturer, when it's not the fault of the public. Their complaint against the public was much like the complaint of the bandit against the rich man—the fellow had money, and this tempted the bandit, and if the rich man hadn't had money, there would have been no banditry.

All this led George Romney, president of American Motors, to make a curious remark:

"I have found dealers," he said, "as a group, are just as honest and just as farsighted as manufacturers."

General Motors' Harlow Curtice didn't see matters in this same, reasonable light. He came scorching to Washington, called the dealers a pack of liars, blamed them for bootlegging and assorted evils, denied everything, and said that General Motors never pushed an unwanted product on anybody.

Then, a bit later, Mr. Curtice returned to Washington a calmer man. The gist of his new testimony was that he wanted to take back some of the hard things he'd said. He explained, in the homely turn of phrase that so often characterizes the speech of General Motors officials, that it had since occurred to him "that where there was smoke, there must be some fire." It turned out there *was* something in what the dealers had been saying, but now, Mr. Curtice said, he'd investigated, made "suggestions," and that new "policies and practices that all agreed were reasonable and practical" had been adopted, and no legislation was therefore necessary, thank you.

There was now in effect, Mr. Curtice said, a new formula that would convert the manufacturer-dealer relationship into a lilting song. Meanwhile, he conceded General Motors *had* condoned price packing, but said pressure from competition had forced GM into this disreputable, reprehensible practice. The competition, apparently, consisted of the fact that General Motors sold only slightly more than 50% of all the cars sold in America. One can imagine Mr. Curtice's hurt astonishment to find that almost five of every ten buyers were purchasing either a Ford, or a Chrysler, or a Studebaker-Packard, or an American Motors, or a foreign product, instead of wisely buying Mr. Curtice's own. A thing like that can shake any honest workman's faith in himself.

Henry Ford II, president of Old Henry's empire, followed Mr. Curtice to the stand to explain that a lot of curious things must have happened—if they happened—while he was out of the office. But all that, Mr. Ford said, was bygones. He, too, was going to help dealers to a new plane of finer understanding. Like Mr. Curtice, Mr. Ford did not, and would not condone misleading advertising and spurious sales practices by dealers, if discovered. Like Mr. Curtice, Mr. Ford saw little need for legislation.

In short, the manufacturers' reply to the indictment was exemplary, fully worthy of them, and if anything remains now to be desired, it might be that the manufacturers' eyesight for dealers' frauds could be improved, because six years after Tom Wretch struck his bargain with Bob Joy; three years after the Senate hearings; the plain pack, the top pack, the finance pack, the bush, the switch, the highball, the lowball, the boot-legging, the usury, the unhorsing, the unsecured loan and the grand competition are still as much with us as the blitz and the quaintly scented advertising.

The only real changes in the bazaar since Tom Wretch was last there are that the prices are higher and the noise level is several decibels lower, because the crowd is smaller. The entertainment and the wares remain the same.

"Detroit's answer to overproduction or slow sales is kind of interesting," one dealer explained. "It used to be the law of supply and demand said if you get too much supply for the demand, what you do is lower the price. What Detroit does is cut production and *raise* the price. They just kind of amended the law of supply and demand so they'll always get theirs."

The crowd at the bazaar is slimmer because Tom Wretch hasn't come back in great numbers this year. He's still trying to pay for that Stylepack Super he bought in 1953. He re-financed his note in 1955, 1956, and in 1957. A good many other souls have left the bazaar's chrome-plated Midway to go across the street to look at the small cultural exhibits from Europe.

Wretch will be back soon, however, because we remember he bought more than a pack when he bought that Stylepack. He bought dynamic obsolescence with a vengeance, for not only is he sick of looking at his 1953 car, but now, in 1958, it's coming apart. In a way, it is wonderful to contemplate how a piece of machinery that cost Wretch $2,589.90 could, in five years, come to be worth nothing to Wretch and only about $100 to a used car dealer.

Let's not consider the finance charges Wretch paid. Let's merely estimate the allowances for depreciation, and the cost of insurance, license fees and taxes, gasoline, oil, tires, grease, repairs, cleaning, and the money Wretch tied up in a non-paying investment. We discover that it costs Wretch $.1042 to drive his car one mile.* Since Wretch drove 12,000 miles a year for five years, we discover it cost him at least $6,252 to acquire and drive a car for five years, or $1,250 a year.

This is absurd, of course. How can a man spend $1,250 a year on an automobile when he earns only $3,900 a year?

He can't.

But he does.

His family goes without new clothing and they buy three pounds of hamburg for a dollar and that's their supply of meat for the week, and Mae Wretch gets a part-time job and so the little Wretches go without parents, but, by George, the Wretch family has a car. It is the focal point of their lives.

Very well, we will admit their lives are somewhat out of focus, and I'd go so far as to say who are we to try to save the Wretches from themselves? Still, these admissions do nothing to banish the gamey flavor of the entire business we have been considering thus far. Let's shove Wretch aside and ask these general questions:

Where is the morality in two, or two hundred prices for the same automobile? What effect do you think this kind of pricing has on all other merchandising? The automobile, central to our economy, is the most expensive so-called necessity any-

---

* The current average operating cost for a car priced at $2,300.

146

one can buy except a house. If it has no price, what else can have a price?

Where is the morality in selling a car to a man who is obviously incapable of paying for it unless he is willing to deprive his family of many necessities? Where, for that matter, is the morality in burdening an oaf with a debt, simply because he is an oaf? What effect do you think this sort of sale has had on the sale of all other things to the public, except to make our national economy more unstable and our business morality in general even more whimsical than it is?

But wait—we are not through. Tom Wretch is not the end of a line, but the beginning of one. When Wretch walked from Honor Bright's door, twirling the keys to his new car, he was startled to find Bob Joy standing beside his old car, talking to a young man with sideburns and a black leather jacket.

"I know you won't believe it," Joy was saying, "but God help me, it's the truth. This car had only one owner, a retired schoolteacher. She never drove it except back and forth, up and down her driveway, on alternate Sunday afternoons in the summer. Only reason she turned it in was that a kid had busted that window with a rock. It's a late '50 and we gave the full $1,500 for it. Tell you what—we'll split the difference, because we have to move the used cars we're taking in today. It's yours for $750, and we can work out a nothing-down deal and give you $300 in cash besides. . . ."

At this point, it should be understood that dealers do a larger business in used cars than in new cars, and Honor Bright is no exception. About two-thirds of all Americans buy old or new cars on time; on trade-in and installment. Wretch buys a new car; Doe buys his old car; Roe buys the old wreck Doe traded in, and meanwhile turns in a fourth car himself. One new car is sold, and somewhere along the line, one old car is led to the junkpile and meanwhile, nobody really owns any of them except, perhaps, the junk dealer. All along the line cars are sold to people who can't afford them; to people who must pay with promises instead of cash, and so the entire economy of the automobile industry is secured by promissory notes. But what secures the notes? Only a long line of automobiles, all unpaid for, moving toward a junkyard. As Lloyd Morris points out in *Not So Long Ago* (Random House, N.Y., 1949) each car in the procession is so far removed from the note it secures that nobody cares where it happens to be, or who has it at the moment. The procession, he said, supports the promissory notes exactly as the gold at Fort Knox supports the national credit—nobody's really seen it, but everybody believes it's there, and thus a national faith in a junkyard-bound stream of cars that no one owns ultimately keeps the assembly lines humming in Detroit.

"Somewhere along that dismal road," Mr. Morris says, "even very poor Americans [are] able to intercept cars that they could afford to buy— on the installment plan. They paid more for these cars than they were worth; so had the dealers who originally accepted them as trade-ins. For it was not to the industry's advantage to permit a cash—and competitive—market in used cars; such a market would inevitably depress prices to a point where Joe Doakes might find it more advantageous to buy a good used car than a new one."

Here, we might pause to reflect that Mr. Charles Wilson, late of General Motors, late of the Defense Department, remarked that what is good for General Motors is good for the country, and vice versa. This might strike some people as a rather parochial viewpoint, because what is good for General Motors is obviously installment buying, but the net effect of buying automobiles on time might be to contract, not to expand, the national economy. Briefly, if Wretch and his wife go without food, clothing, shelter, cleanliness and medical services in order to swing the note on the new Stylepack, the effect is that all the people providing the Wretches with food, clothing, shelter and sundry goods and services, will fare worse. In theory and in practice, the manufacture and sale of automobiles is an index of prosperity. Because the automobile industry is the heart of our economy; because so many jobs are dependent on the industry in all its ramifications; it is true that employment and wages are at high levels when many automobiles are sold. But if buying an automobile means the customer not only pays for an overpriced car, but also assumes a staggering debt, the money he pays out on his debt cannot be spent for anything else. Thus, there is less money available for butcher and baker. Thus, presumably, butcher and baker are less able to buy or to operate cars. Thus, presumably again, fewer cars are made and sold and driven; thus the economy contracts. The facts would seem to indicate that when one perches on a spiral, one can either spiral up or spiral down.

Well, exploring fiscal jungles is apt to be fun, and it's too bad we don't have more time for it in this weighty tome. Other matters are more pressing, however. We recall that Tom Wretch paid out an awful lot of money, thinking he was buying a car with it. Seldom in the history of recorded thought has an opinion been more mistaken. The car Wretch bought represents only a fraction of the price he paid for it, because Wretch was not only handed a pack, and then a bill for a machine which was already obsolescent, but a bill which also covered the cost of cowboy suits that nobody wanted to wear.

Cowboy suits?

Certainly. Cowboy suits and ten-gallon hats. And not only cowboy suits, but also ponies, hotel bills, girls, lies and slip covers. Let's run along to the next chapter to see what it was that Wretch *really* bought when he visited that Oriental bazaar.

S.O.B. DETROIT

ASK Tom Wretch how much his new car cost, and he'll tell you what he paid for it. Ask him what his car is worth, and he'll give you the same figure. Tom means well, and he has answered you as best he can, but price, cost and value are seldom synonymous, and nowhere is this truism more apparent than in the automobile business. Besides, Tom had no way of knowing that the price of his Stylepack Super included charges for tools he would never see or use, slipcovers never installed on his or anyone's car, railroad freight charges never paid to any railroad, magazines no one read, diamond rings, manufacturers' mistakes and taxes. Indeed, nearly two-thirds of the price Tom paid went for things other than the cost of the materials and labor that built the car, and some of these extra things were downright esoteric—Indian headdresses, for instance.

It must be said that Tom Wretch was deeply satisfied with his purchase, and he thought he'd struck a bargain. Still, he couldn't really understand why a 1953 automobile should sell for three times the price of a 1941 automobile. To be sure, he thought the '53 model a somewhat better car, but he was not completely convinced that it was three times better. Tom put the question thus:

"Why the hell these goddamn things cost so much?"

A good question. We shall try to answer it in detail, beginning with the plight of Simon Greed. It must not be thought that Greed is a barracuda, lancing through the water to snap up tiny fish like Tom Wretch. It is more accurate to envision Greed as a middle-sized fish, eternally fleeing the grinning dentures behind him, gulping down little fish like Tom in a desperate attempt to keep up his strength for his perpetual flight. In fact, Mr. Greed's blitz, while a happy inspiration, could almost be considered an inspiration born of necessity. There was one day, some weeks before the sale, when everything seemed to happen to Greed at once; when the teeth behind came terribly close. The day began with Honor Bright's service chief, Walter Wrench, coming into Mr. Greed's office to say:

"Hey, boss, we got some more of those do-it-yourself kits outside."

"My God, not again?" Greed pleaded.

"Yeah," Wrench said. "Real dogs."

The last of the new cars had been unloaded and the truck trailers had gone. There were cars with doors that did not fit. There were cars with vital parts chucked in on the back seat floors, like afterthoughts, which is exactly what they were. There were cars with missing parts. There were cars with wind-

Detroit sitting on the dealers

shields that leaked; cars that would not budge an inch under their own power. Simon Greed felt a familiar, sharp pain in region of his wallet.

"How bad is it this time?" he wanted to know.

"About five days a car," Wrench told him.

For the hundredth time, Greed wondered how and why any factory could offer slapped-together, unfinished products for retail sale. Sweater factories did not send half-knitted sweaters to clothing shops. Bakeries did not sell half-baked pies. Detroit, however, not only turned out unfinished automobiles, but did not bother to *offer* them for sale. Detroit *told* Greed how many cars Greed was to sell, and Greed had to take what he was sent, under threat of loss of franchise. If the cars were sent out with leaky windshields, Greed was to seal the windshields. Gloomily, Greed estimated his current shipment would tie up a considerable part of his service department for a week, merely readying his wares for sale, and Greed would have to pass the cost of this on to his customers as a "handling charge." It irritated Greed to charge his customers for the factory's mistakes, but there was no way out for Greed. He shrugged and walked back to his office.

The telephone was ringing.

"Simon?" a jeering voice inquired. "Jack. I'm in the Lazar House. Can you get here at ten sharp? Fine. See you."

Jack was Jack Smiles, General Chrysford's zone sales manager. The Lazar House was a shiny cube of concrete, stainless steel and neon tubing, Metropolis' newest hotel. Jack always stayed there when he came to town. When Jack said Jump! a hundred dealers leaped high in the air, Simon Greed among them. When Jack said Crawl! a hundred dealers writhed on the floor. Jack never visited a dealer's office, but summoned the dealer to his hotel.

"This is Bill," Jack told Greed, jerking his head in the general direction of a desiccated gnome in one corner of the room. "Bill—Simon. Simon—Bill Fiscal.

"Bill is going to go over your books," Jack said. "There's a lot of crap in your operation, Greed, and we're going to straighten you out. . . ."

During the next two hours, Simon Greed learned once again how futile it is for any automobile dealer to imagine himself to be the owner of an independent business. Bill Fiscal told him, for instance, that General Chrysford dealers must adhere to a uniform accounting system, despite the fact that if Greed followed it, Greed's books would tell a lie, and that Greed would wind up paying more Federal taxes than he owed. Here, Greed ran into the same situation that a former General Motors dealer complained about to the United States Senate.

"We understand the value of uniform accounting to obtain valuable comparative figures," the dealer testified, "but we also believe our books should reflect the truth of our operation, not just to show the largest profit for the moment. We came to the conclusion that the GM accounting system was 'cocked' to reflect the highest profit from new-car sales, and that a dealer could go bankrupt with his books lying to him and showing a profit. For this reason we made certain changes so that if we were losing money our books would reflect the fact and we would have the opportunity to correct what was wrong."

The result of "making certain changes" was that General Motors began jumping up and down on him, the dealer said, despite the fact that the United States Internal Revenue Department said the dealer was right and that General Motors was wrong.

"As it now stands," the dealer said, "every dealer who follows the [GM] manual . . . is needlessly paying more taxes than he should. We would estimate—in the over-all GM dealer picture—it would run into millions of lost dollars. We cannot conceive GM handling their own tax accounts so loosely."

Greed had to put up with this kind of thing from Bill Fiscal, and to put up with a lot more besides from Jack Smiles. In short, Greed was told he would have to make capital improvements on his shop and office, despite Greed's plea that his service facilities were already adequate, and so was his office room. He was told he would be billed for a General Chrysford magazine that would be sent to his customers. He was billed for advertising and window trim that did him no good; advertising which was placed at a higher rate than Greed would have paid. He was told where he could buy his office stationery. He was told to pack prices to the extent of $450 a car. He was compelled to buy a year's supply of seatcovers, windshield washes, tailpipe extensions, gas tank guards, cushion toppers, back seat radio speakers, spotlights, bumper guards and other odds and ends that Greed simply could not sell to his customers.

Jack Smiles told Greed that General Chrysford thought Greed should be selling more parts and service—that Greed's mechanics should be finding more things wrong with cars brought in for service. Greed was made to buy duplicate tools and machinery. If he wanted to buy a particular tool, he couldn't buy that tool alone, but had to buy a whole package of which that tool was just one part. The new models, Greed was told, demanded different tools, and so he would also have to buy a supply of this year's tools to service this year's cars despite the fact that last year's tools would do the job. As one dealer complained to the Senate:

"They bend them [in this case, wrenches] a little bit differently so it looks different in the picture, but the opening is the same."

And, as Senator A. S. Mike Monroney added, "the air-conditioning units are so made that you have to have a certain type of gadget or part for a left-hand compressor and a right-hand compressor, which in service operation requires [the dealer] to increase literally by many percent the stock of parts that he has to have for all of the new things that are hung onto the cars. . . ."

Greed was also told to chip in for prizes to be handed out in dealers' sales campaigns. He learned from Smiles that if he, Greed, wanted to sell out at any time, General Chrysford would find him a buyer and set the sales price. He was told how many cars he would be expected to sell, and discovered he'd have to pay for them on shipment, and not on delivery, no matter what the state of his cash-on-hand.

Once again, Greed was reminded—as he was reminded every year by Mr. Smiles—that the factory was under no compulsion to send him any cars to sell.

The trouble was, Greed had signed a one-way contract when he accepted a General Chrysford franchise. The factory could tell Greed what Greed would have to do, and if Greed didn't do it, the implication was clear that he would no longer be a dealer. Jack Smiles knew this very well, and this is why he could treat Greed with disdain, and why Senator Monroney was able to say that zone sales managers like Smiles wrote dealers the kind of letters "you wouldn't write to a dog."

Even if Greed had needed the amount or kind of advertising, office stationery, tools and parts that Smiles rammed down his throat, Greed was in no position to shop for them in an open market. He was told from whom he could buy these things, and since many of the checks went to General Chrysford, it seemed to Greed (and to a good many other dealers) that the suppliers were in cahoots with the automobile manufacturers.

Greed nodded and smiled and said, "Sure, Jack," and, "Thanks, Jack, I see where I was wrong," and, "Yes, sir, Jack, I sure will," as Smiles went mercilessly on and on. This was the same Jack Smiles for whom Simon had helped other dealers to buy Christmas and birthday presents. Simon, and other dealers in Smiles' zone, had so far bought Jack's wife a grand piano; Jack's son a Palamino horse; Jack a diamond ring and cases of whisky. When Jack would inevitably leave to move to another satrapy, giving way to another predator, the dealers would buy him a going-away present.

"And one more thing," Jack told Greed. "You're coming to the zone meeting, right? And this is what you'll wear . . ."

The zone meeting would be held in a town 200 miles away, to introduce new models, and dealers would not only chip in to

support the show, but would also make something of a show of themselves. It turned out that dealers from Greed's state would be dressed as Indians. Dealers from Tennessee would come in coonskin caps and backwoods costumes; Texans would wear cowboy suits and brand-new ten gallon hats. Greed and his second-in-command, Bob Joy, would order their Indian suits from Nepotism Costumes, Inc., but the check would go to General Chrysford Corporation. Each Indian suit would cost

159

$125, and would be worn just one day. Greed and Joy would be under no direct compulsion to attend, any more than Greed was under any compulsion to be an automobile dealer, but somehow, as Smiles talked on, Greed gathered the distinct impression his absence would be noted. Greed felt the same way about it as did a fellow dealer who told the Senate:

"I can tell you how our zone forced Buick dealers to buy monkey suits at $125 each for one day's use at the meeting in which the new models were announced. I used the word 'forced' there with this definition in mind: 'You buy the suit like every other dealer in this zone so you can be part of the team and help us to make a good public showing for Buick in this region or zone.' "

For his own reasons, Simon Greed very much wanted to be thought a worth-while member of the General Chrysford team.

When Smiles finished giving Greed the benefit of his advice, he thrust a cold hand toward Greed and said:

" 'Bye, Simon, nice seeing you again."

Smiles jerked his head again at Fiscal, who obediently put on his hat and left the room with Greed. Greed and Fiscal rode to Honor Bright's shop in silence. While Fiscal spent the afternoon prying through Greed's books, Greed listlessly ate a ham sandwich and drank cold coffee from a paper cup, and idly looked at his mail. The first letter, from General Chrysford, told him what his share of the coming year's advertising campaign would be. Some part of Greed's money would help to put a young lady in evening dress atop the hood of a new General Chrysford coupé, which would spin slowly on a turntable beneath a floodlight at the New York automobile show, two thousand miles from the closest of Greed's customers. Greed sighed.

The next letter told him what his quota of General Chrysford's new Luxury Super-Novas would be. As usual, it was too high. The Super-Nova was the longest, widest, lowest, most luxurious dreamboat manufactured by anyone, and there weren't two men in Metropolis who, by any stretch of the imagination, would want one at the wholesale price. Greed sighed again. He'd sell his Super-Novas at a loss and make it up by packing the price of his less expensive models. It was the only thing he could do.

If you somehow deduce that each of Greed's sighs cost Tom Wretch a few dollars, you are absolutely correct. Tom's share of Greed's advertising bill, for instance, would be $35. There is no question that had Simon Greed—and many another dealer in this nation—been an independent businessman in fact, Tom's car would have cost Tom less. If Greed could have kept economical books; if he could have ordered only the number and kind of automobiles he could best sell in Metropolis; if he could have been his own best judge of his need for capital investment, office supplies, parts, tools, gadgets, advertising and costumes; if he could have been his own judge of how to run his business in his part of the world; if his automobiles had come to him in running order, then he could—and would—have charged Tom less.

As it was, Tom Wretch did not want slipcovers. Slipcovers were therefore not installed on his Stylepack Super. Simon Greed, however, had to buy slipcovers for Tom's car, whether Tom wanted them or not, and so part of the money Tom paid

161

covered the cost of the slipcovers that Greed bought. Thus, one part of the complicated answer to Tom's innocent question, "Why the hell these goddamn things cost so much?" is now apparent. Wretch was paying for an unnecessary overhead that the manufacturer ordered Greed to incur.

Tom Wretch also paid for freight that weighed nothing and never moved. It simply did not exist. The manufacturer charged Greed for it first, and Greed sighed, and Tom Wretch picked up the bill. This is another minor matter to be sure, but a host of such minor matters runs into fairly important money. The Interstate Commerce Commission, for instance, says the Detroit manufacturers turned a tidy $200,000,000 profit each year from the "phantom freight" charges Tom ultimately paid.

When Tom bought his car, the practice was for the manufacturer to estimate the freight charge on a finished automobile moving from Detroit to the dealer's showroom, but estimating the charge on the rail rate per mile multiplied by the airline distance. If any freight charges were actually paid, however, they were paid by the manufacturer on the unassembled elements of a car, moving from Detroit to a sub-assembly plant in the dealer's area, and on the finished car moving from the sub-assembly plant to the showroom. The cost of shipping pieces is far less than the cost of shipping a finished automobile. The manufacturers simply charged the full freight rate of the finished automobile, paid the actual cost of shipping the pieces, and pocketed the difference.

But wait—not all the components of an automobile are necessarily manufactured in Detroit. There may be parts factories within a state shipping to a sub-assembly plant within that state. In such a case, nothing moves from Detroit at all; the only item moving in interstate commerce is the customer's money. Well, the automobile business is full of such little surprises, and if you like surprises, you will be pleased to learn that not only did Tom Wretch's car not come from Detroit in any shape at all, but that it traveled neither by air nor by rail. It was wholly built within Tom's state and arrived at Simon Greed's door on a truck.

The United States Senate heard testimony that the profit on this kind of operation was used to build more sub-assembly plants, thus risking the customer's money, and not the manufacturer's, for capital investment. Judging from his remarks during the lengthy hearings, Senator Monroney seemed to feel that the net effect of such a building program was that the customer paid the manufacturer a premium to achieve a position from which the manufacturer could more efficiently fleece the customer.

Not everyone could be charged FOB Detroit, phantom or real, however, because the rail freight on a finished automobile arriving in California would have put the retail price somewhere in the neighborhood of the national debt. Therefore, West Coast customers were charged much less for freight than the actual cost. The result was that East Coast purchasers paid relatively more than did West Coast purchasers in order that the same car might be offered on both coasts for roughly the same retail price. Thus, the New York customer paid the manufacturer a premium in order to permit the manufacturer to sell a car to a Californian for less money than the Californian would have expected to pay, had the freight charge been levied.

At the Senate hearings, Detroit defended phantom freight

on grounds that it would be an economic impossibility to charge a customer an honest bill for freight if, at the same time, you were to try to arrive at a standard retail price for a national product. There would be different prices for the same car in different states; indeed, different prices for the same car within the state; and the result would be unimaginable marketing chaos. Phantom freight, Detroit said, was just one means of canceling everything out—you could offer the same car for the same retail price everywhere, and Detroit would lose money sending cars to California, but recoup it by sales in New York. Nevertheless, Detroit's spokesmen admitted, phantom freight as currently practiced did seem to have its little contradictions, and therefore Detroit was now dropping it. Tom Wretch, it seems, was one of the last customers to be parted from his money by just this means. Now, Detroit told the Senate, the whole thing was being resolved. Dealers were no longer charged rail rates unless the cars reached them by rail; if the car came by barge or truck, barge or truck rates would be charged. Yet, Detroit was not ready to abandon some kind of scheme for balancing out the Californian loss, compensated by the New York overcharge, without also abandoning a national retail price schedule. Therefore, the reduction of phantom freight charges would take the form (1) of using much the same old method but hiding the charges in production cost and (2) alleging that the new, higher price of the new car simply reflected how much better a car it was.

It may truly be as Detroit claims—that no better freight charging system can be devised. Detroit is trying to establish what is known as a basing point for national freight. A thousand other firms use the same general method in transcontinental business. There is nothing illegal in such a scheme, and in many ways it is altogether admirable. What irritated some Senators was the way in which Detroit used the scheme to make a *profit* of nearly a quarter-billion dollars a year. If, in balancing out the freight rate costs to achieve a national retail price, Detroit broke even, then we could say there was value offered for value received. But when a profit is made which has nothing to do with either cost or effort, then there is value received for no value offered; a toll is levied for a service not rendered. Certainly, such a profit cannot in all honesty be considered a production cost. It must be said that Detroit is constantly seeking a more equitable basing point formula, and it would be good to believe Detroit's efforts were not inspired by Interstate Commerce Commission belchings, but proceeded from a simple love of one's fellow man. The fact remains, however, that the freight charge a customer now pays does not represent the actual freight costs incurred by Detroit and dealer in marketing the car. This is a minor matter, costing the customer few dollars. The sum of such minor matters, however, helps us to answer Tom Wretch's question.

If the manufacturer's relationships with its dealers seem sometimes to be a bit overwhelming, as General Chrysford's were with Greed, and if its freight charges seem somewhat devious, the manufacturer's way of arriving at his wholesale price is downright slippery. Another part of the answer to Tom Wretch's plaintive question is that automobile prices seem to be set more by greed, whim and opportunity than by cost, supply and demand. Few formulae have more variables than that

165

followed by manufacturers in arriving at a wholesale price. Detroit calls the formula the "standard volume concept" and this is how it works:

The factory guesses how many cars it can make during 180 to 190 working days a year.* The production during these days is called the "standard volume." The manufacturer now estimates how much it will cost him to make that number of cars. This figure, of course, ranges farther afield than the simple costs of material and labor.

Next, the manufacturer decides to set an arbitrary rate of profit that will allow him not only a profit on this year's business, but will also provide a mattress against an uncomfortable year. Twenty per cent is the kind of good, round number that Detroit understands. A round number has the special quality of being able to roll in any direction you wish. So, our manufacturer adds a 20% profit to his estimated *cost of production*.

Comes now the nagging matter of taxes. If you and I make any money this year, we pay our taxes out of what we earn. It just goes to show you that we're in the wrong business, because in Detroit, it is the customer who pays the manufacturer's taxes for him. The automobile maker figures what taxes he'll have to pay—and adds *this* to his production cost.

Next, the manufacturer divides the total of the figure he's now reached by the number of cars to be produced during the standard days, adds in the Federal excise tax of 10%, and calls the result his wholesale price. If he sells fewer cars than

---

* In almost anyone else's calendar, there are some 260 such days, but Detroit allows for all sorts of stray factors, such as an uneven production flow, and other matters which concern us not.

he turns out in his standard volume days, his profit shrinks. If he sells more, it's all giddy gravy to be spooned around to corporation executives in the form of bonuses and perhaps to stockholders in the form of extra dividends.

At this point, it is easy to see the wholesale price could be as padded as a traveling salesman's expense account and as elastic as his conscience. Obviously, the key to the matter is the cost of production, and this is impossible for any outsider to determine for the simple reason that manufacturers rightly say this is their business and nobody else's. We can remark that figuring the cost of production must be a fascinating pursuit even for the manufacturers, however, inasmuch as their business is so curious that they can claim an anticipated profit to be one part of the cost of production.

Briefly, the manufacturers answer Tom Wretch's question by saying the cost of labor and materials has steadily increased, and that's why the wholesale price has increased. By July, 1957, the wholesale price of passenger cars was 36.4% higher than 1947 prices, an Automobile Manufacturers Association spokesman said. At the same time, the AMA man went on, the cost of tires increased 52.4%, steel increased 81.5%, metal-working machinery cost 66% more and small cutting tools were up 51.8%. The cost of labor is 95% of the production cost of a car, according to the same source, and the cost of labor increased 50% in that decade. Besides, the AMA spokesman continued, let's look at it this way: a car wholesaling at $1,800 in 1949 would cost $2,225 today; but wages have increased. It took the average factory worker 32.8 weeks of work to earn the price of that '49 car, but today, it takes him only 27.5 weeks to earn enough to buy a "comparable, though far superior car," the spokesman said.

Taxes have increased, the AMA man said. Also, he said, if steel goes up $10 a ton, the factory pays between $20 and $25 more because of all the middlemen who handle steel between the steel mill and the Detroit factory. The cost of styling changes and fancier gadgets must be passed on, the AMA says, because the public demands that styles and gadgets change and improve from year to year. It is only because of such demand, the AMA says, that such odds and ends as clocks and turn signals are no longer optional but standard equipment on many cars. Besides, the AMA says, the profits are not exorbitant. In its biggest sales year, General Motors made about $257 on every car, before taxes. If $100 were cut from the price of every $2,000 car, one Detroit spokesman said, the maker would have to sell 130,000 more cars in a million-car year to make up the sacrifice, and, he said, he didn't think 130,000 more customers would be attracted by so small a reduction in price. Furthermore, the manufacturers argue, if we expand our plants, then we're entitled to a larger return because the investment on which a profit must be made has now increased. If such expansion were really subsidized by the customer, instead of being risked by the investor, then—Detroit argues—the motor companies wouldn't be nearly a billion dollars in hock to the banks as they claim to be.

This sort of chitter-chatter leaves Walter Reuther cold. Mr. Reuther is president of the United Auto Workers, and while there is no intention here of becoming involved in a labor-management dispute, we might remark that labor thinks the AMA has not told the whole truth. Mr. Reuther's basic position is that greed has more to do with the price of a car than has the cost of labor. While the union has not inspected the manufacturers' books, it says there seems to be no free wholesale market; that the dealers are a captive market, paying the manufacturers' price, or else. Further, Mr. Reuther thinks more than coincidence is involved in the nearly identical prices of different makes of comparable automobiles. The UAW claims that higher wages have been more than offset by automation and mechanical improvements that have increased worker production; that General Motors' lowest profit on investment after taxes was 19.9% in 1956; that the average after-tax profit percentage of all other United States manufacturers is one-third to one-half lower than Ford's and General Motors'. The union also believes the cost of labor and materials lags behind price increases, and takes great joy in quoting Mr. Charles Wilson to this effect. Mr. Wilson was General Motors president when he wrote in the September, 1952, *Reader's Digest* that: "I contend that we should not say the *wage*-price spiral. We should say the *price*-wage spiral. For it is not primarily wages that push up prices. It is primarily prices that *pull* up wages." The italics, the union says, are Mr. Wilson's.

While labor and management bicker about such trifles, there seems no doubt that the cost of labor and materials has increased, and keeps on increasing, and so do taxes. Whether the manufacturers are as humble as they say they are, or whether they are as greedy as Mr. Reuther thinks they are, is a matter of taste. There is no doubt that automobile prices keep going up, and there is a surprising unanimity among labor, management, dealers and anyone else however remotely concerned with the automobile business that styling is chiefly accountable for increased production costs.

The cost of styling changes for the 1958 automobiles was so high, *Popular Science* said in late 1957, that without spending a cent more for the next two years, Detroit will have to charge each customer $100 more for his car in each of two big six-and-a-half-million car sales years, in order to pay for it. It seems fairly obvious at this writing that 1958 will not be one of those years, and sundry forecasters say that 1959 won't be one, either. It should be remembered that Detroit's usual answer to a poor sales year is to increase the price of the cars. Thus, Detroit hopes to recover its cost of 1958 model styling during 1958 and '59, the customer will pay more than $100 for his different tail fins.

At this point, dealers and manufacturers at last clasp hands over the consumer's grave. They agree there is just one reason for those expensive styling cycles—the public. Their feeling is borne out, *Popular Science* said, by the fact that in 1949, 22% of all cars sold were in the lowest price bracket, while in 1957, only 11.5% fell into this bracket and the majority of those sales were to fleet buyers. In 1956, the low price division of one manufacturer figured the public would buy 10% of its premium cars, only to be astonished to find its gadget-laden dreamboats comprised 30% of the total sale. Since this kind of music has haunted our little tome, it might be well to look into the cost of styling to such extent that Detroit will lift the veil. Since chromium trim seems to be synonymous in Detroit with industrial design, let's wonder about the trim on Tom Wretch's new Stylepack Super.

A large part of the price Tom paid for his chromium bumper guard had—naturally—nothing to do with either the cost of the chromium or with the salary of the man who put it on the car, or with the salary of the man who decided where it should go. Instead, Tom's money helped to pay the cast of a kind of perpetual Keystone Kop comedy which bemuses Detroit night and day. The November 4, 1957, *Time* magazine reported "Over all the styling studios hangs a curtain of near-nuclear-plant secrecy.

"Ford's fifteen studios have locks that can be changed in half an hour. A security force of twenty guards run by an ex-FBI agent checks every employee's badge (a different color for each division) to make sure that no one is where he should not be. Outside, the security patrol has a sixty-power telescope to keep watch on a nearby grain elevator where rival spotters might lurk. All unused sketches are carefully burned; all experimental clay models smashed. Everywhere, posters exhort the stylists to keep mum about their work. Samples: 'No matter where, talk with care'; 'Don't foretell the future.' "

Each company employs elaborate stratagems to penetrate the other companies' styling secrets—there are paid spies and counterspies; rumor-placers and counter-rumorists. In all this desperate hugger-muggery of burned plans and smashed models, there is just about everything you'll find in an Eric Ambler novel except a genuine sense of humor, although the end result is laughable enough. Briefly, the spies succeed, despite the guards. All designs are alike, anyway. Nothing is unknown. As market research director David Wallace said two years ago, "All companies have each other's designs as far ahead as 1959." Thus, the only concrete meaning Detroit's slapstick security farce has it that the customer pays for it, along with that strip of chromium he may or may not want.

The customer also pays for things like Chevrolet's investigation of its own sounds and smells, and apparently the customer paid the Ford company, in its chief designer's own word, "millions" of dollars to discover a rug just like the rug in Mom's living room. One wonders why so. If you're looking for a rug just like Mom's, why not go out and buy one from the same store that sold one to Mom, instead of spending millions on a long shopping tour? The claim will be made, of course, that the rug in the car must look like Mom's, but be made of something else. Often a search for what Fred Allen used to call "a reasonably accurate hand-drawn facsimile"

172

can run into the millions that Ford says it can, which brings up the matter of the executive's wife and the two-way stretch.

A friend in the textile business tells us that a fabric company, experimenting to discover a new upholstery cloth for Ford, came up with a plastic mesh that stretched under the weight of the sitter. When the sitter stood up, the thing bounced back together again, and the idea was, the cloth

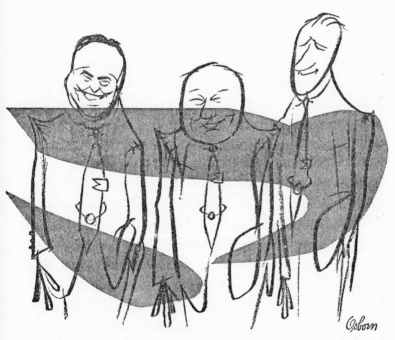

The not too original disorderizors!

173

would stretch two ways rather than wear out. There was just one minor problem. The cloth had been sat upon by buttocks clad in every conceivable material, and it turned out that if a woman wearing mink or sable sat on the cloth, the guard hair of the furs would penetrate the interstices opened in the stretched cloth, and that when the lady's weight was removed, the cloth would spring back faster than the guard hair could be withdrawn, and the furs would once again be trapped.

This effect was observed only with mink or sable, however, and so the Ford company, no doubt figuring that few Ford owners would wear such exotic furs, installed the new cloth on a new car. One of the car's first occupants, however, was the sable-clad wife of a Ford executive. Down she sat. Interstices appeared; guard hairs penetrated. Up she rose. Interstices closed; guard hairs were caught. She kept on rising, and in the process, tore all the fur out of the seat of her coat, and presented to the world much the spectacle of a half-apsed cathedral.

The fabric was rejected and research proceeded.

Well, fun and games of this sort are expensive, and so are $50,000 offices for design chieftains, and even more expensive is the retooling necessary to produce not a better body design, but merely a slightly different wrinkle in a fender. Also expensive are the multitudinous gadgets which seem designed not so much from the standpoint of utility, but with an eye to creating the kind of novelty that leads to a sales talk. Since a sales advantage, rather than any other advantage, is what Detroit seems to be seeking in its design departments, let us consider this matter.

There was a time when an automobile's electrical equipment was quite simple. A battery operated the starter, the headlights, cowl lights and rear lights. This permitted the car to start, to see and to be seen in the dark. To achieve more or less the same effects, the battery of a currently popular automobile now operates four headlights; two stop lights; two tail lights; parking and signal lights (2); dome lights (2); courtesy lights; rear license light; beam indicator light; shift indicator light; light switch "escutcheon" lamp; ignition switch escutcheon lamp; ash tray light; cigar lighter and cigar lighter light; heater control light; instrument cluster lights; glove compartment light; parking brake warning light; temperature indicator light; turn signal indicator lights (2); electric clock; electric clock light; underhood light; rear compartment light; back-up lights (2); radio dial light; spotlight; hand spotlight; trunk and utility light; starter; fuel gauge; oil pressure warning light; generator warning light; ignition switches; radio; heater; air conditioner; window motors; seat adjustment motor; defroster fan motor; radio antenna motor; automatic radar light dimmer; windshield wipers. Optional equipment to be operated electrically includes radio-telephone; back seat television and an ice-making unit.

This sort of gew-gawry not only helps to make cars fantastically expensive without adding much either to convenience or to performance, but it also makes upkeep exorbitant. When anything breaks these days, it breaks expensively. If, for instance, your old hand-cranked window stuck, it was a simple job to go inside the door to fix it yourself. Today, you not only pay an expert in a white suit to take the door apart, but you have to subsidize an electrical engineer to wrestle with a mass of multi-colored spaghetti before he can find the wire that leads him to begin to make his diagnosis. When or if he finds the trouble, his usual advice is to buy a new electric window motor.

And what, pray tell, is the advantage of a window that moves up and down electrically? The only stories pouring in from the newsfronts of the world across this busy desk indicate that electrical windows are perverse. In the coldest Vermont winter of many a year, a Cadillac's electrical windows jammed open. In the middle of a Dallas heat wave, an Oldsmobile's jammed shut. In Philadelphia, a child, fiddling with the pushbuttons, caught one hand and yelled bloody murder for the next three hours and six minutes.

Why are power brakes necessary if not to stop the overpowered car? Why do we have power steering, if not to overcome the difficulty of parking bigger, fatter tires on a heavier car? Power steering can throw a novice off the road and power brakes can hurl him through the windshield.

Electrical widgets, greater speed, more power, power brakes, power steering and buttons to push all, add up to advertising copy, however, and as *Fortune* magazine remarked in August, 1953, the "propensity to spend, indeed, is likely to depend for a long time on those practitioners of persuasion, the sales and advertising men."

In other words, when you spend money for styling, you do not necessarily buy the efforts of competent industrial designers—you buy the designers' adaptions of the contributions of the advertising writers, ever a gimmick-minded lot.

And here, as in so many areas in this fascinating business, you don't get what you think you're paying for, because much that glitters in an advertisement is simply absent from the automobile. The advertised horsepower, for instance, is based on "test stand ratings."

It must not be imagined that Detroit's "test stands" actually test anything that lies within the realm of common experience. What is tested, so to speak, is the power of the engine alone, unconnected to transmission, driveline, differential, axle, wheels and tires. Further, the test takes place under idyllic conditions not to be found on any road. The engine is mounted on a dynamometer block in a clean, well-lighted room where it is soothed by abundant, carefully cooled air. A slight vacuum is created in order that there shall be no exhaust back pressure to hamper the happy scamper of the pistons. There is neither fanbelt nor radiator; hence the engine does not have to turn so much as a generator. The spark is adjusted by hand at every change of speed to give the rosiest of figures on the dials, even though this usually causes the engine to knock so heavily that it sounds like an infantry division demonstrating rapid musket fire. Finally, when the tests are complete, the advertising department gets to work. Therefore, an engine advertised as 300 horsepower might, by standards other than those of the dynamometer block and the advertising department, turn up 100 horsepower less, and sometimes more than 200 horsepower less. One veteran dealer, whose father had been mechanic and dealer before him, sourly watched a "300 horsepower" dreamboat glide by. "If that thing has more than a sixty-horse engine," he said, "I'll eat it."

177

Hence, it is a fact, if a rather cold and uncomfortable one, that when we try to tell Tom Wretch why his car cost so much, we must include the salaries of liars. The problem still remains, which came first, the liar or the victim? Or, to put it another way, Who makes taste? The public, or Detroit? If the public bites on the advertising bait, does this constitute entrapment, or a "public demand" for styling? A moot point. Suffice it to say it's all very expensive.

By this time, I'm sure you'll be glad to know that approximately one-fourth of Tom Wretch's money went neither to dealer nor to manufacturer, but to the Federal and state governments. The sum of Federal taxes on a $2,000 car in 1953 was $434.17 in Detroit. This is something Tom can do nothing about, without capturing control of Congress, and the manufacturer simply adds it to his production cost in figuring his wholesale price. The total Federal and state tax on one of the so-called low-price cars today is apt to equal the entire retail purchase price of a low-priced automobile in 1941.*

Thus, the tax collector does his little bit, and provides another part of the answer to Tom's question as to why the hell these goddamn things cost so much. Meantime, please recall that Tom Wretch confuses the price he paid with the worth of his car, and that price and value usually have little connection with each other. Actually, Tom's gadget-hung Stylepack Super had one value to Tom, another to Simon Greed, another to the General Chrysford Corporation, and still another

---

* A two-door Ford cost some $641 in Pennsylvania in 1941; this is the approximate tax in Pennsylvania today on some models of "the low-priced three."

to the credit company that bought Tom's paper.* Likewise, Tom's automobile would have a fifth value to you and a sixth to me, which is to say, it had no objective value at all.

Moreover, Tom's car would have no value to anyone but a junk man if it didn't run. Obviously, it would seem that the essential value of an automobile is that it moves under its own power, but this value changes even if the efficiency of the machine remains constant. For instance, if Tom kept his Stylepack Super in top-hole shape for seven years—if to all intents and purposes the thing ran as well seven years later as on the day he bought it—Tom could not realize more than a junk price if he were to try to sell it outright. For curious and altogether untenable reasons, an automobile is presumed to depreciate faster than a saucer of milk on a sunny porch in August.

Since the value of a car has little to do with the functional ability of the machine, but is largely a figment of the purchaser's imagination, it is idle to try to define it. In passing, however, we might reflect that everyone believes that all our automobiles have some sort of value to someone else, and even if no one knows what that is, the *belief itself* is what makes the installment plan possible and keeps the entire industry functioning. This unfounded belief is the kind of thing a President calls "confidence."

It is easy to see that Tom Wretch boated about on a murky

---

* That these values are intangible is disclosed by the fact that, in the mid-1950s, a group of banks financing automobile sales asked the National Bankers Association to provide some kind of formula that would establish a correct market value for the automobiles that secured the notes, but good answer came there none.

sea of drifting prices and nebulous values, buffeted by the winds of advertising. As result, he had not too much choice. Still, had he been a somewhat better sailor, he would not have lost so much, because there is a way whereby the customer can come upon something resembling a standard price for an automobile and thus bring price and value somewhere within hailing distance of each other. Let's suppose you, no Tom Wretch, are going to buy a new car. This is how you do it:

You know how the manufacturer's wholesale price is set, and you know there is nothing to be done about *that*. But you also know something Tom Wretch did not. You know that this wholesale price is not the same to all dealers, nor does it remain constant to any one dealer throughout the model year. At the end of a model year, when dealers are unloading what is now last year's dog to make room for the all-new dreamboat that is shortly forthcoming, the manufacturer often cuts his wholesale price. In other words, if you pay at the end of the model year the same retail price that obtained at the beginning of it, you've probably been stung because the wholesale price probably dropped.

And remember: if you are trying to buy an automobile, and not an illusion, the car you buy at the end of a model year is just as factory-new as the car you would buy on the first day of that year. You know, also, that the dealer can charge you whatever he thinks he can, no matter what the wholesale price. Moreover, it is not always well to believe a dealer when he says, "Honest, Mister, I'm giving this to you at only ten bucks over my wholesale cost"—and then shows you a figure which purports to be the manufacturer's price—because not only may the wholesale price have dropped by the end of the year, but also because factories often give discounts of more than $100 a car to sprightly dealers.

If you have spies in the automobile business, or are otherwise privy to the secrets of the dealers' safes, you can estimate the general retail price in your area. To the state and local taxes, add what the dealer charges to put the cars in running order. Then add his freight charge, topping your total with one-third of the dealer's wholesale cost to serve as a good guess on his gross profit before expenses. You have now established your basic bargaining position with the dealer, and from there on, you're on your own. In event you do not pay spies, and are not adept at cracking safes, there is still another means whereby you can create some kind of standard price in this dank situation. Unlike Tom Wretch, you close your ears to local advertising.

You know the car you want; let's say it is the cheapest four-door sedan that General Chrysford makes. You visit at least five General Chrysford dealers in your area and give each the same song and dance. You have no car to trade in. You are going to pay cash. You want the cheapest car, painted black, without extra equipment of any kind—no heater, no ash trays. You certainly do not want an automatic transmission. Further, you don't care how long you'll have to wait for delivery. Having said this much, you now ask the price.

Once you've established the basic price of the stripped car, you are then free to bargain for any gadgets you wish to add. If a dealer says, "I can't give this to you by itself, because it comes as part of a package deal that included a Kleenex dispenser," you are entitled to laugh at him. The automobile dealers of today are the horsetraders of yesterday, and you have to keep your hands in your pockets to keep theirs out.

No doubt you are not going to pay cash for your new car; this is a little white lie you tell the dealer. You are going to finance your car through a bank, not through the dealer, but the effect is that the dealer gets the cash. Thus, you have already denied him one of his chief means of profit—insurance and finance charges. If he is a horsetrader, he's one step ahead of you, and he may have automatically compensated by quoting you a packed figure as his rock-bottom price of that stripped-down car. This is one reason why it is well to go to many dealers with the same story. You may not find them far apart in their prices, but at least you will have established some kind of standard retail price for your town. Your next step is to squeeze any possible pack out of that price.

"Every dealer will charge you all he can," one dealer confided. "I can give you twenty-five to twenty-eight per cent off my suggested list price—which is an honest price—and still make an honest deal."

He paused.

"I'd say twenty-five per cent off would be an honest deal," he repeated, retreating 3% as though by reflex action. "A man's a sucker to pay the list price."

Asked what was so "honest" about a price that was 25% higher than an "honest" price, the dealer explained:

"It's the kind of list price you see around. But I'll be fair. I have to make $200 on each of forty cars a year to break even on new car sales. But I can get a hundred per cent absorption of my overhead on my service department. Seventy-five to eighty percent absorption on service is a good figure; some of us get a hundred per cent. And I'm not exactly giving my used cars away. So a guy comes in, and he wants a deal, and I figure what the hell, I'll give him something off because he may have more money another year, and anyhow it's another car out of the shop and off the quota, so I give him twenty-five per cent off: So then the next guy comes in, he wants the convertible and I sell him everything but my secretary on a three-year paper, and I make it all back and maybe another buck besides.

"All a guy has to do is ask me," the dealer said, "and he's got a new price to think about. The guy I hate to see is the guy who comes in and he asks how much, and I tell him, and what do you know, he's got his pen out and he's signing a check.

"I didn't know he was going to pay cash. Nobody could have known. So I had this finance charge in the price I gave him. Now, what am I going to say? Tell him the price was packed? Tell him the list price was packed? If I told him that, he'd tear up the check and tell everybody I'm a crook. If I let him go ahead and pay the price, and he finds out he's been packed, he's going to tell everybody I'm a crook. With a guy like that, I have to say, Gee, don't you know we can get you a better deal than that, and he says, Gosh, no, he never heard of it. Of course he never heard of it, because I just made it up out of my hat, right there, but I yank the pack out and sell him the car. If he'd asked harder, I could also have given him that twenty-five per cent off I was talking about, but why bother? He's happy; he thinks he's made a deal; and I'm happy because all of a sudden I'm not a crook any more."

If everyone followed the pattern of buying outlined above, we would very shortly know just how many people *demand* two tones, white sidewalls, electrical high chairs, automatic windows, chromium schmaltz, automatic transmissions and so on. All we know at the moment is how many people *buy* them, which is another way of saying we know how many people can be sold these things. If, unlike Tom Wretch, you and I and the man down the street do not fall for misleading advertising and packed package deals, but tried to buy only that which was worth while to us, and drove our bargains, we would not only set a price, but fix a less nebulous value and, at the same time, create a style. All this, of course, is based on the preposterous assumption that we want or need a car in the first place. We probably don't need one at all. More-over, there isn't any place worth driving a car, even if we had one, as the next exciting chapter will clearly show.

THE CALL OF THE OPEN ROAD

ALL ADVERTISEMENTS show automobiles in unusual circumstances. They depict smiling, handsome people in evening clothes arriving in glittering hardtops beneath the portecocheres of expensive tropical saloons. A polished convertible, top down, filled with laughing young people in yachting costumes, whispers along an idealized shoreline. A ruggedly healthy Mom, Pop, Sis and Buzz smile the miles away as their strangely dustless station wagon whisks over the Rockies. Sometimes, automobiles strangely shine on pedestals; sometimes they slip through astral voids like comets. None of the advertisements show you and me in the automobile as most of us know it—that is, wedged in a fuming line of commuter traffic at 8:30 A.M., or locked in an even worse outbound line at 6 P.M.

A manufacturer, of course, would commit economic hara-kiri if he were to try to sell us a car on truthful grounds, for how could he ask anyone to pay $4,500 for a three-hundred-horsepower contraption on grounds that it would be used only two hours a day for 240 working days a year, and would at all other times—except briefly, on vacations—be parked in an expensive parking lot or sit depreciating at a curb? Would you buy such a car if it were truthfully put to you that the thing would cost you more than $9 an hour to use? No manufacturer in his right mind would plead with you to buy a luggage compartment only slightly smaller than Delaware in order that you could use part of this space just twice a year. Manufacturers know very well that the American automobile is not primarily a means of transportation and that it cannot be sold as such. Therefore, their advertisements invariably portray the automobile As Flying Carpet—as a thing to sweep us off to ineffable lotus lands—and this, we discover, is the greatest lie of all. Yet, we cannot plead surprise, because— as a friend remarked— if we now suspect that our automobiles are overblown, overpriced monstrosities built by oafs for thieves to sell to mental defectives, it is only logical to expect that there is not much point in driving them, and that any place an automobile can go is probably not worth visiting. Nevertheless, the advertisements have a certain appeal, because the dream they represent once had substance. There was a time in man's memory when travel was exciting.

186

The OPEN road

R.G.

It is difficult to say just when the last shred of fun disappeared from the American highway. Some people think it was in 1927, when Henry Ford stopped making the Model T, but other authorities put the date in the late 1930s when the first national restaurant chains spread like plague. Speculation is idle, because we must accept things as they are, and there is no question today but that family travel in America is apt to be one of life's more crashing bores. Let me wipe off the lens a bit for a quick look at two generations of the Foresight family:

Early in the 19th century, Abel Foresight, his wife, Hope, and their children, Prudence, Faith and Jonah, set out from Morgantown, Pennsylvania, in a wagon. They chopped through forests, crept over mountains, forded floods, shot their suppers, struggled with savages, and trusted in God and in their strength to cross an unknown continent. They were more than a year en route, but the Foresight family arrived in California with the look of eagles in their eyes. Theirs was the age of travel adventure.

In the summer of 1958, Roger Foresight followed the path of his longfathers across his native land.

"We take the car it's cheaper," he told his wife June, in the curious English of his day. "You don't see the country you take the train or fly."

Whereupon, Roger gripped the Deep-Dish Command Wheel of his twenty-foot-long Flite-Flo Hacienda Wagon, stirred the Jet-Boom Eight's Power-Plus into life, pressed a master button that wound up all the Saf-T-Tint windows, adjusted the Koolaire to a desired temperature, pushed another button to bring the Flote-Fome seat to its proper level and distance, pressed yet another to cut in the Glyde-Ryde Dynamatic Turbo-mission, and swung away from his Cape Cod Tri-Level's Kar Porte to begin three thousand miles of driving pleasure.

A week later, the Foresights arrived on the opposite coast a little tired from sitting so long on foam rubber, but otherwise they were quite the same people who had left home. There was still that look of vague disappointment in their eyes, because Roger and June Foresight dwell in the tasteless, or Pablum, stage of family travel.

Several springs feed Roger Foresight's sense of disappointment. Even after the West was subdued and the automobile devised, there was a time when motoring was not dull and tasteless, and together with many Americans, Roger Foresight can remember it. Therefore, we can say that today's realities disappoint Foresight's memories. Next, we can say his disappointment was inevitable because Foresight was dead wrong in three major assumptions. He was wrong in imagining there might be some significant difference between New York and San Francisco, or indeed, that there might be any fundamental differences among any American cities. Oh, there are plenty of superficial differences, to be sure. San Francisco has hills and a lovely harbor and New York does not. Denver has a magnificent public park system and Chicago is simply a blot on the landscape. The point, however, is that the cultural anthropology of our cities is much the same; the life of the average citizen of City A is very like the life of the citizen of City B because the ecology of one big town is quite like that of any other, particularly in a nation of standard brands, chain stores and national fads. Neither you, nor I, nor Roger Foresight would be able to tell whether we were in Philadelphia or New York if we joined a crowd of shoppers in Gimbels, because the shoppers in Gimbels Philadelphia store look exactly like the shoppers in Gimbels New York store and come from the same economic classes, have the same kind of jobs and entertain much the same hopes of Eternity. No doubt there are many reasons for this situation, but one of the more massive seems to be the automobile, as we'll see in a moment. Meanwhile, allow me to suggest that Roger Foresight was also wrong in thinking he'd see more of the American continent if he drove. He was also hopelessly wrong in assuming that driving across the nation would be cheaper than flying or taking a train. Here are matters that merit investigation, so let's dispose of the easiest of them first, giving Roger Foresight the benefit of every doubt, even if he might not deserve it. Consider the matter of cost:

We remember the current national average operating cost of a $2,300 automobile is $.1042 per mile; thus the cost of driving the 3,030 miles between New York and San Francisco would be $315.72. (Roger's Flite-Flo Hacienda Wagon is a dreamboat in the $4,500 class, and it costs a good deal more than this to run, but we're going to give Roger all the breaks and use the low average figure.) He will have to drive 473 miles a day to make the trip in a week. If we can possibly imagine that he and June together can spend only $9 a day for food and only $5 a night for lodgings, it will cost them a rock-bottom $413.72 to make the trip—one way.*

The cost of two Pullman berths—lower berths—for the same trip is $374.62, and the Foresights would be only three days in transit. Even when we consider the outrageous prices of railroad dining car meals, and the necessary tips to porters, it would be cheaper for the Foresights to take the train.

An airline will sell Roger two one-way tickets from New York to San Francisco for $317.70, one meal included, and the trip takes half a day.

If we further presume the Foresights will return, we must note that there is no round-trip saving if they drive, but that there is a substantial round-trip saving on air or rail transportation. Purely for argument's sake, let's say that driving is no strain on the Foresights, and that time is no object. They are as insensate as two bags of wool. Even if we grant this preposterous assumption, the economics of the thing indicate the Foresights are silly to drive unless, perhaps, they like to throw their money away. Some people do. In fact, we find them buying Flite-Flo Hacienda Wagons. Nevertheless, we might imagine Roger Foresight to be a little disappointed to find that his trip cost him more than he had thought it would.

The major reason for the lackluster look in the Foresights'

---

* Obviously, few people would—yet some do—drive across the country in a week. I use seven days here to indicate this is the shortest possible time it would take you to drive if you traveled approximately 500 miles a day instead of setting a killing pace. The point to be made is that transcontinental driving is neither saving of time nor money.

To simplify the arithmetic in both regards, I've presumed the Foresights have no children. If you want to give them three kids, please reduce the driving time to include tinkle stops, imagine the traumatic experience of being cooped up in a car with three babies all howling at once, and add what you will for food and lodging.

eyes, however, was their discovery that it is now possible to drive across the face of the nation without feeling you've been anywhere or that you've done anything. The Foresights remembered the first days of the twentieth century, when most Americans lived out their modest lives within five miles of the rumpsprung hamlets of their births. In those days, there was difference and variety in the land. Tennessee's troubadors were mercifully pent within Tennessee's forgotten hills, and did not wail and whine from every jukebox. A visible, palpable cultural distinction then existed between Philadelphia and Chicago. In 1900, a man could cross the nation and smell different smells, taste different foods, hear different accents and be cheated by different methods. Driving anywhere was almost as much of a demanding adventure as was waddling along in Abel's wagon. The hardy motorist took joy in being his own mechanic, and he was ever watchful for signs of trouble among the natives, for in those days rustics buried rakes tines-up in the dust of country lanes to puncture the tires of the devil-carts that frightened the horses.

As the automobile became more general, the various tumult of our native land subsided, and now that nearly everyone has at least one car, scarcely one American in fifteen lives anywhere near his birthplace, and Americans drift about their continent as easily as tumbleweeds, and with as much sense of direction or purpose. No matter. Like tumbleweeds, they may expect to find a congenial ecology wherever they go; one Howard Johnson restaurant is exactly like all the others.

If you fly across the nation, it is still possible to observe some variety, because you look down on a geological exhibit.

192

The bones of the land are still apparent from ten thousand feet up. You can see rivers eating through the plains; see the mountains thrusting up from the dead shores of unknown epiric seas. At a convenient altitude, it is still possible to sense the majesty of old Abel Foresight's accomplishment; you are overwhelmed by America's space.

If you take the train, you have not the same Olympian perspective, but you can see more of the country than if you drive, because you rattle along miles of open landscape and you have some opportunity to look at it, for your view is not blocked by billboards and your attention is not commanded by the demands of the road.

The road. Ah yes, the road. Let us think of *this* together, you and I.

For centuries, "road" was a word of magic. Armies, gypsies, beggars, tinkers, peasants, merchants, highwaymen, scholars, minstrels and runaway apprentice boys were once found upon the road. As recently as fifty years ago, you could still build your house beside the road and be a friend to man, because mankind passed your doors. Today, this is not so. The road belongs entirely to the automobile, and he who builds his house beside it can only watch the Fords go by, because there is no human life on the road itself. Indeed, so mechanical, so abstract, so inhuman have our roads become that American drivers never think of passing the people ahead; they think of passing the car ahead.

If this point seems somewhat frivolous to us, it is by no means frivolous to occasional visitors from less peppy lands where horsepower is still a word relating to the power of a

193

horse, and where the word "road" still has connotations of Pilgrim's Progress, or of the royal road to romance. Last year, America was host to one Dan Jacobson, a South African, who expressed his sense of bewilderment to the editors of *The Reporter* magazine.

"The six and eight lanes of traffic are flung into swathes of tar and concrete that fill the sky in loops and curves dwarfing even the city beneath them," Mr. Jacobson wrote. "There the roofs of the cars, curved like the wing cases of beetles, flash above the concrete parapets in a hundred different colors; there are no shops there, no billboards, there are no people and nowhere for people to walk but a kind of narrow catwalk along the side of the parapet where a man can clamber to the emergency telephones if his car breaks down. There, where there is no place for a man outside his moving car, the road reaches its purest, most abstracted state—it can be used for nothing but to carry cars from one end of its giant structures to the other. The colors are black and gray; from afar it is desolate and beautiful, but unlike a natural desert, it has no peace. . . ."

Significantly enough, Mr. Jacobson at no point suggests that man has anything to do with the road—not even with its creation. He reflects the road's sole concession to animal life is a catwalk—but this leads only to the telephone that summons help for the broken car. Mr. Jacobson was talking about the superhighway, or Autobahn, which is the road's ultimate abstraction, serving cars, not men. As the automobile evolved from Tin Lizzie to the overblown Cleopatra's barge we see today, she demanded wider, smoother, straighter roads, and

every human juice was distilled from road building in order to accommodate the desires of the automobiles. The automobiles' demands constantly multiply faster than we can build Autobahns, however, and thus traffic engineers say that the U.S. Government's plans for new superhighways to be completed by the end of 1975 are already hopelessly inadequate in terms of the number and kind of automobile Detroit expects to spew forth in the next *twelve* years. Therefore, if our automania persists, we shall ever need ever wider roads and the townless superhighway, desolate as the desert Mr. Jacobson says it is, is clearly the shape of our future. A part of Roger Foresight's transcontinental journey was undertaken on such a road, and this is how it was for him:

His left leg kept falling to sleep because there was nothing for his left foot to do in the pushbutton Flite-Flo Hacienda Wagon. His neck grew stiff from having to hold his head fixed straight ahead as he stared down the endlessly unrolling straight strip of black tarmac. Traveling at speed, he dared not take his eyes from it. The banked, graded, militarily landscaped road was identical for all its fantastic length, and thus there was no new thing to entrance June Foresight's idle eyes. On this road, a thing as monotonous as an indoor track built for six-day bicycle races, the Foresights had no idea of miles because the scenery never changed. Thus, they kept track of time. It was so many hours from one town to another; from one service area to the next. All the service areas, with their uniform gas pumps and their identical restaurants and their identical jittery travelers, served to illustrate the proposition that America has achieved a peculiarly high degree of standardization in our time. Modern Americans that they were, it did not occur to June and Roger Foresight that there was anything odd in classifying food as a service.

The Foresights passed each Autobahn night in a neon-lit AAA-approved motel that was exactly like the motel of the night before and like the motel of the night to come, and thanks to television in every room, the Foresights never missed an instant of Mark Sade's coast-to-coast quiz show,  *Can You Take It?* All along the everlasting monotony of the Autobahn, the same national voices beat into the Foresights' ears during the day, thanks to the miracle of the Flite-Flo's radio. Thus, Roger and June were spared the burden of having to think of something to say to each other as they hurtled across the continent, but even for souls more lost than they, a ride on the Autobahn is apt to be a journey in Limbo. No one can say it is in any way a pleasure to sit like a lump for endless hours while one speeds along in a vacuum, and no one does. Instead, the Foresights—and every other American user of Autobahns—say that *where* they want to go is far more important than the act of *going there*. This statement not only strips travel of at least half its pleasure, but it is as ironical as it is pitiful, as we will very shortly see.

Meanwhile, it is clear that not all American roads are Autobahns, but our secondary highways are just as devoted to the needs of the automobile. They are distinguished from

Autobahns by a hardy species of anthropoid life that clings to their edges, just as weeds curiously flourish among the cindery desolation of railroad yards. Here, along the berms, are to be found the proprietors of cut-rate filling stations, the sellers of fried foods, the owners of ice-cream palaces shaped like bulldogs, the concierges of the motels that Mr. J. Edgar Hoover regards as "camps of crime . . . little more than camouflaged brothels," the juke joints that sell knickknacks and balsam-stuffed pillows that say For Mother on one side and Souvenir of Lake On-Wee on the other. Here are the small businessmen who have put away their masks and riding boots to set up roadside garages. Here are the stands that sell hooked rugs, cut bait and plaster garden sculpture all at once. Here are the proprietors of junkyards and the businesses of those who tow broken cars out of the way of the cars that still work. Here are the birds that pick the crocodile's teeth; the pilot fish that flit ahead of the shark; here are the practitioners of twentieth century symbiosis. Here, along the edges of America's highways, is the detritus of our century—the fields of burnt and rusting automobile carapaces; the billboards that suggest the only thing keeping you out of the voluptuous arms of a hot woman is your dreadful stench. Here are the broken beer bottles and the signs that ask you to help keep America green and the signs that strangely hope that Jesus saves. Here, in a word, is U.S. 1—perhaps from Philadelphia to Washington; from the old capital to the new.

The Foresights moved over these roads, too, and discovered that travel along them is merely an endless passage down an indefinitely extended, unplanned Main Street. It is disheartening to admit that America generally accepted the billboards and the brothels, the ice cream and the junk, long before it came to the conclusion that such a street with its innumerable entrances, exits, crossings, pull-offs, winking neon signs and varying speed limits was unsafe for the automobile and should therefore be abandoned. Yet, the fact that the cluttered two-way highway is unsafe is solely responsible for the present transition to the sterile Autobahn, and so we may say that even the last vestige of adventure—physical danger—may disappear from American motoring as our Pablum stage of travel wears on.

When Roger and June Foresight drove across the country, they ever felt time's winged chariot hurrying near, and thus they did not explore the only American roads that are neither boring nor blatant. In short, they did not travel our rural lanes, and it is a pity they did not, for they may never have a chance to see one again. Parochial politicians have already covered most of them with asphalt in a naked bid for the peasant vote, but until quite recently the little roads have been the quiet routes of reapers and wains, and the few automobiles to use them merely carried unsuccessful agriculturalists to the village post offices on the first of the month when the government checks arrive. Today, all this is rapidly changing. The back country roads have been discovered by the rich, who go wistfully popping and bouncing over them in their little foreign cars, still trying to discover the automobile's once-hinted promise of fun.

Unfortunately, the handwriting is on the wall. Within the next ten years, there won't be a lane in the land that lacks its

Jaguar agency, its French restaurant and branch of Abercrombie & Fitch. Next will come the middle classes, aping their betters as is their wont, but demanding wider, straighter roads for their less agile Buicks, and the French restaurants will print menus in English and serve Parker House rolls. The country-day schools will appear, and the rich will be forced once again to search for private amusement in yet another corner of the world. By this time, the lower middle classes will be pushing in, as they do, and the former country lane will be well on the way to becoming the four-lane highway, lined with filling stations and leering with used car lots, connecting the housing development to the shopping center that offers plenty of everything and the best of nothing.

Thus we see that the smaller road, built more to the human scale, is inevitably de-humanized as the volume of traffic increases; the country lane of today is the cluttered highway of tomorrow and the abstract Autobahn of the day after. At this point, the triumph of the automobile is complete and the full attention of driver and passenger is directed to the automobile itself. From this point on, the only possible emotions available to the passengers are boredom or terror.

We note the Autobahn is somewhat safer for the automobile than the cluttered highway, but safety is always a relative term. It should be remembered that our automobiles are not built with safety in mind; quite the contrary; and you put your life in the automobile's trust the moment you leave your driveway, because the car was born accident-prone if not downright bloody-minded. In 1905, for instance, there were only two automobiles in the whole of the sprawling Kansas City area.

Somehow, they managed to find one another and collide. Since then, a national folk saying has grown up, used whenever anyone wishes to cajole anyone else into a dangerous undertaking. The hazard, we say, is no greater "than crossing the street," and everyone knows what we mean. We mean to say the street is damned risky, and you have to have your wits about you to negotiate it in good health, but if you take every precaution and obey all the rules, you might just make it. Indeed, when Roger Foresight drove across America, he ran a much higher risk of disembowelment en route than did his ancestor Abel, who had to contend with the hostiles. It is possible to come to a sticky end at any moment through no fault of your own on the safest of our Autobahns, but as if determined that better roads will not reduce unduly the quality of danger, and so denude happy motoring of its one last thrill, Detroit keeps on producing faster, more powerful cars and shows an equal genius in making them progressively more collapsible. I beg you to recall the not-so-hard tops.

Curiously enough, the increasing power and speed of the automobile contains a contradiction. On the one hand, speed adds a quality of danger, but at the same time, speed helps to make auto travel even more bland, because whatever scenery there might have been between City A and City B passes faster than the passenger's eye can comprehend it, and speed requires the driver's eye to be fixed on the unrelenting road. This is why Keats' Law of Autobahn Travel says the only possible emotions are terror or boredom, depending on the individual phlegm quotient of the traveler, as influenced by speed. We state this mathematically in two formulae:

Let T stand for terror and IPQ for individual phlegm quotient. R stands for rate, or speed, and B for boredom. The formulae will now read: T equals IPQ times R; B equals IPQ divided by R. It will be seen that speed is the crucial factor, no matter what the IPQ.

These formulae most usually apply to visiting Europeans, however, because the IPQ of most Americans is 0. Most Americans, like the Foresights, are content to work out the more familiar formula, Distance equals Rate times Time. Like the Foresights, they never think of, much less try to solve the equation in terms of Distance. They always seek Rate in order to find Time. International marriages often demonstrate conflicts of attitudes, and fortunately we have an example close at hand:

Muriel, an English girl, was only a few days arrived in America when her Yankee bridegroom told her they would have supper the following day with friends who lived thirty miles away. Early the following morning, Muriel began packing for the trip, selecting clothes and putting up a picnic lunch. She envisioned a pleasant outing along placid lanes. She looked forward to savoring new sights; to seeing something of the natives and of their curious customs and dress. Muriel dreamed of a picnic beside a stream at midday; of a little postprandial nap with her love in the shade of the trees; then to taking high tea at an American inn, and ultimately arriving at their hostess' house in time to dress for a champagne supper—staying the night and returning the following day. Now, Muriel is as good at arithmetic as anyone, but it never occurred to her to think of a supper invitation in terms of $D = RT$. She had anticipated a civilized little holiday on the continental order, where the distance to be traveled is something to be explored and enjoyed. Therefore, she was somewhat startled when her bridegroom, used to dividing America's Distance by the automobile's Rate, slipped her the word in terms of Time. He solved the formula in his head, automatically.

"Say, honey," he said, "I got noos for you. It on'y takes fordy minnits to get there."

Now, wiser in the ways of Ammedica, Muriel understands. One does not sup in Ammedica; one eats. One does not cover distance; one travels through time, and the sooner the better, because the distance is such a bore with nothing much to see if the billboards let you see it. Her husband always puts it thus:

"You wanna get there, don't you?"

A new veteran of America's roads, Muriel sometimes agrees with him, but most often she says, "Why don't we just stay home?"

We must admit Muriel has a point, the point being that there isn't much point in going to, or being in any place in America other than where you happen to find yourself at the moment, and we have the automobile to thank for this. We have seen what the automobile has done to the road, but now let's look at what it has done to our cities and to our vacation resorts. Perhaps then we will better understand Muriel's resignation and that dull look of disappointment in the Foresights' eyes.

On their way between New York and San Francisco, Roger and June Foresight passed through Cleveland, Chicago, Hannibal, St. Joseph, Denver, Salt Lake City, Reno and Sacramento. They could tell when they were leaving a town because little pennants began to appear on the gasoline stations at the city limits, and when the Foresights next saw pennants on gas stations, they realized they were approaching another city— not a new city, mind you, but just another one.

Had the Foresights wished, they might have reflected that a curious kind of national square dance goes on night and day in downtown Cleveland, in downtown Denver, in downtown Anywhere, U.S.A. Stop! the lights say, and twenty million automobiles jerk to a halt. Walk! the lights say, and seventy million pedestrians obey. Go! the lights say, and twenty million automobiles lurch ahead. Necks snap, eyes pop, legs flex, lights blink, whistles blow, horns honk, fumes choke, and we call this civilization. From time to time we are asked to defend it.

Obviously, this civilization is exclusively designed to meet the demands of our automobiles, and since all automobiles have the same demands, all our cities are built alike. All of them tend to become as inhuman and as abstract as the Autobahn that struck poor Mr. Jacobson all of a heap.

It remained for *Yank*—a soldier-edited, Army-sponsored magazine—to drive the point home during World War II. Thinking to remind the brave soldier boys of Mom, Sis, and the Girl Next Door, *Yank* decided to run pictures of sundry American Main Streets. Several hundred photographs were selected, whereupon one sly editor suggested running a number of uncaptioned photographs on the same page, challenging the readers correctly to identify their home towns. The venture was a morbid success, for devil a soldier could find devil a bit of difference among the pictures, and the nasty suspicion grew that *Yank* had merely taken several snapshots of the same street full of automobiles from several minutely different angles. Few believed *Yank's* answer to its puzzle was on the up-and-up.

If all our downtowns are somewhat surrealistic landscapes populated by automobile-dominated automatons, what can we say of the suburban housing developments which fester around the edges of these civic wounds? Here are mantraps as devoid of originality as anything that ever rolled  off a Detroit assembly line. Here, too, are robot populations that are slaves to the automobiles that make the developments possible in the first place. A housing development anywhere is—in two dirty words—a car pool.

If in traveling from coast to coast, the Foresights had merely seen more mechanical roads, more mechanical Main Streets, more mass-produced suburbs and more mechanical people riding in machines to their mechanical tasks, we might reasonably expect them to be entitled to a little routine disappointment on discovering that New York is just a larger version of San Francisco, except for superficial, or detailed differences, particularly if they had misty memories that some kind of real difference once existed. They might have wondered, privately, if their trip had really been necessary. All this is as easy for us to see as it is discouraging, but wait—a more mas-

205

sive disappointment clamors for attention. Suppose the Foresights had more than seven days to spend on themselves. Let's
say they floated free as disembodied spirits, seeking out those
lotus lands the automobile advertisements seem to guarantee
as part of the purchase price. Let us imagine the Foresights at
Cape Cod.

On Cape Cod, the Foresights found the natives much the
same as natives anywhere else in America—the Cape Codders'
beady little eyes glittered through their glasses as they smiled
the empty smile of commerce and made change at their cash
registers. The tourists were gaudy blotches of color moving on
crowded sidewalks; there was a honk of horns in the street;
there was a frenzy of fat ladies in shorts and thin ladies in
dirndls; a coming and going of paunchy, knock-kneed men in
Bermuda shorts and polo shirts. There were up-tilted sun-
glasses everywhere, and shops where you could buy souvenir
postcards of places you had never seen and would never visit,
and other postcards that built little jests around the presence
of wasps in the outhouse. Cape Cod was a flow of hot children,
an ebb of exhausted mothers, a drift of people walking in between people who were taking pictures of each other. Cape
Cod was waves of juke boxes, Coca-Cola, suntan lotion, high
prices, sand in the shoes, twenty-three flavors of ice cream
and there was one peculiar odor which, from time to time, ate
through the grease smoke of the restaurants and the exhaust
fumes of the automobiles. A child asked, "What's 'at funny
smell?"

"It's the sea," his mother explained.

At Ausable Chasm, there was not the disquieting smell of

the sea, but a fungus-scent of damp growths in the narrow gorge, and girls seeking immortality added their names in lipstick to the thousand other names on the rocky walls. Otherwise, the Foresights found Ausable Chasm to be like Cape Cod in all significant respects, and when they drove to the top of Mount Washington, they found the same tourists, the same natives, the same indigestibles, and the same souvenir postcards a few thousand feet above sea level.

Of course, the Foresights could have gone to the Catskills where the planned entertainment is so well planned that nobody has a chance to be alone or to do anything but follow the leader through a round of merriment that includes wearing funny hats and blowing tinsel horns. Or, they could have gone to the Golden West, to join the fantastic line of automobiles slowly inching along the precipice of Yellowstone Canyon. Or, perhaps, they could have sought out some sylvan retreat in Minnesota, to join the hundreds of other people who were either water-skiing on the lake or throwing beer cans into it.

It would not matter where the Foresights drove to their vacation. The scenes everywhere are much the same, because where one automobile can go, all other automobiles *do* go, and wherever the automobile goes, the automobile's version of civilization surely follows. To be sure, there are still some vacation resorts not yet in a stage of full development, but there are none in a stage of *arrested* development.

Twenty years ago, the slogan, See America First, still had some point. Nowadays, the fact is that if you've seen one part of America, you've seen it all. The automobile did not put the adventure of travel within reach of the common man. Instead, *it first gave him the opportunity to make himself more and more common,* so that when he reached the point in his development where he could find leisure for travel, the lotus lands had disappeared *because he was already there.*

Still, it cannot be said that the common man knows this. We find him constantly trying to pretend otherwise. Who, for instance, do you think really is in that advertised hardtop that swirls to a stop beneath the porte-cochere of the expensive tropical saloon?

Queen Marie of Roumania?

No.

It is merely Roger and June Foresight, or perhaps even Tom and Mae Wretch, listlessly fetching up at one more deadfall—this one in Miami—there to try to escape for a few numbing hours from the fantastic boredom of aimless wandering in the automobile age. They seek surcease in the familiar national joys of tough steaks, cigarette smoke, watered drinks, insolent service, padded bills and a noisy band.

Man, they say, is really living it up these days.

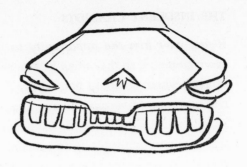

YES SIR, SHE'S YOUR BABY NOW

THERE IS ALWAYS A TIME in the course of a public argument like this when some oaf in the back of the hall stands up and bellows: "Well, if you're so smart, whadda ya' goin' do about it?" Whereupon, the critic on the stage is dumbstruck, not by the ferocity of the reproach, but by its essential merit.

The only fair answer to such a question is to turn it back upon the questioner and everyone else in the hall.

Before we commit this necessary discourtesy, let us suppose —for a moment—that our earth was suddenly buried, like Pompeii, under a vast, instantaneous fall of volcanic ash. All our books, magazines and newspapers were destroyed, but everything else was perfectly preserved. Then, visitors arrive from another planet. In the course of digging a well, they come upon one of our buried cities. What would their archaeologists think of us?

209

The visitors would probably conclude that we were physically so weak that we could not walk ten feet unaided, and therefore built automobiles to carry us about. They might legitimately suppose we worshiped the forces that led us to build automobiles, and that we thus made our machines in the images of our gods. They would assign us different names. In what had been Texas, they would find evidence of the Tail Fin People. In Europe there had lived the Rear Engine People, traces of whom were also to be found on the American eastern seaboard. Pondering the meanings of our metal road signs—Keep in Center Lane, No Left Turn, Slów Children At Play, Street Closed, Dead End, Bridge Out, No Passing, No Parking At Any Time, etc.—they would write monographs on "Tabus of Motor Worship."

These archaeologists would correctly identify a buried supermarket with food, and would probably deduce that it was the site of a curious religious harvest festival at which time baskets of votive foods were superstitiously placed in parked cars. Adults only, and only such adults properly qualified by scientific training, and who further had a demonstrable need to do research in the field, would be permitted to investigate the site of an ancient drive-in theater. Here, where the hot ash had preserved for all time the casts of human adolescents, was obviously the scene of vernal orgy. The chance discovery of an old junkyard would lead to the presumption that ritual burnings of automobiles were held in order that the miraculous rebirth of the automobile gods would take place. Such conclusions would be entirely permissible, if not more or less accurate.

the fake U.S.
culture.

(Orbm)

No doubt some readers may suppose I have occasionally used a fairly long stick to beat a fairly dead horse in the course of this work, but the facts indicate that we live in a land where the politicians are willing to spend more money for new highways than they are willing to budget for all the suggested health, education and welfare programs combined. This would seem to indicate we are building a nation for automobiles rather than one for people. If this is true—and I think it is—then it is not up to one man to suggest panaceas from the rostrum. It is quite enough for him to toot his horn (if you'll pardon the particular cliché) and call attention to what is really public business, and ask everyone in the hall to think about it.

Sober reflection should lead us to conclude that the basic idea of an automobile is good. The idea has grand possibilities, providing that we realize the automobile is after all a machine, and not a love-object, and that we relate its use to some of its proper functions and to some human values. For instance, Mr. Lewis Mumford, writer and city planner, thinks our current automobiles are more a source of chaos than they are a convenience. Speaking to the Thirteenth International Congress of Local Authorities at The Hague on 12 June, 1957, Mr. Mumford said:

"Either the motor car will drive us all out of our cities or the cities will have to drive out the motor car—not by absolute prohibition, of course, but by restrictions of size and access, favoring small cars little bigger than baby carriages, like certain new Italian cars, and penalizing such monstrosities as those fantastic and insolent chariots with which American motor car manufacturers now burden our streets and parking lots."

Mr. Mumford correctly described our automobiles as "the most inefficient and costly of all forms of public transportation."

Significantly enough, Mr. Mumford, as reported in *The New York Times*, was the only one of the day's four speakers to be interrupted by applause. It came just after he made the points above.

Mr. Mumford is not alone in his conclusions. There is a move afoot in Philadelphia to charge people $40 a year for the privilege of parking on the street in front of their houses. The idea is to use the money to build off-street parking facilities, and thus enable the streets better to absorb the flood of moving traffic. In Fort Worth, Texas, it has been suggested to keep cars entirely out of the center of town, and to make the downtown area a pedestrian mall. People driving to the city would park on fringe parking lots nearest their city destinations and there would be moving sidewalks for those unwilling or unable to take the three to four minute hike from the perimeter parking lot to the store or office they wish to visit. Truck deliveries would be made underground. Other city planners propose such things as special lanes for buses; one-way streets; multiple-deck, wholly automatic parking garages with elevators, and requiring new midtown buildings to include plans for off-street parking for their future tenants.

The common factor in this kind of planning, however, is that it presumes nearly everyone will own a car and drive it to town, and that we should therefore change the shape of our cities to accommodate the automobiles. At this point, two major suggestions are heard. One says the small car is an helpful answer to city congestion. The other says it's silly for a city dweller to own an automobile in the first place, and that there should be rapid, constant public transportation from the suburbs. Let's examine these arguments in turn.

Any city planner who thinks that easing the traffic flow will decrease the city's congestion is simply living in a dream world. Likewise, the addition of parking facilities will not, and never has, eliminated parking problems. The rule is, the bigger the road, the more cars. When you improve a small congested road, you wind up with a big congested road. Likewise, the better the traffic pattern, the more traffic on that pattern; the more parking lots, the more people looking for a place to park. Why this should be so is a complete mystery, but there it is—a scientific law as relentless as geometric progression. Similarly, any idea that the small car is the answer to downtown traffic and parking problems is equally dangerous. There is no question of the small car's allure, but even if Detroit answered the anguished request of New York's mayor to make smaller cars, would this *really* mean that New York would suddenly acquire more miles of usable streets? Would not the more probable result be that a lot of small cars would suddenly fill a place which heretofore had been filled with fewer big cars, but that the lack of space between bumpers would remain the same?

There is no use pretending that any city's traffic problems will be ended until (1) the situation becomes positively unbearable and demands a radical operation, or (2) until people

214

begin acting sensibly. While the first alternative is clearly more probable than the second, let's suppose—just for the fun of it—that more and more people begin asking themselves why they had cars, anyway.

It would immediately occur to the arithmetically minded city dweller that it is cheaper to take a taxicab to and from the office every day, and to rent a car for week ends and for a two-week vacation, than it is to own an automobile for a year. If more people realized that it was humanly possible—and often more enjoyable—to walk to some of the places to which they now drive, more of the burden would be taken off our city streets. Indeed, if most city people began really to wonder, Is *This* Trip Necessary? every time they climbed into their automobiles, fewer cars would be sold; the less congestion we should have.

Commuter trains and buses would reduce a city's traffic problems—but only if the suburban public could see that taking the train is cheaper and more convenient and comfortable than driving to town. There's a man in Connecticut, for example, who drives to his New York City job every day. He knows he averages 20 miles an hour in the rush hour traffic at the best of times. He knows the train averages 14 miles an hour faster. He knows it would be cheaper to take the train, because his automobile costs him nearly 12¢ a mile to own and use. Yet, he drives to work. Why?

"Mainly," he said, "I don't like public transportation. If there's going to be transportation, let's have it private. Besides, my car is a lot more comfortable than any seat on that square-wheeled railroad."

So, he comes to the office badly in need of coffee, jittery and irritable from his matutional bout with the traffic, but still thinking he's been more comfortable in his car than he would have been on the train. He thinks that driving his car means he's not part of a public transportation system, when in fact the sole difference between himself and a train rider is that the one is fighting traffic every inch of the way while the other spends the same miles reading the morning paper. Otherwise, neither has real privacy nor freedom of action. Both are sitting in New York-bound machines, with other sitters in the endless line before and behind them.

If anyone is to change that man's mind, it is himself.

Meanwhile, we observe this about cities now served by commuter trains: The railroads, nearing the bottoms of their last buckets of red ink because of many reasons which have little to do with the subject of this work, reduce commuter service as more and more suburbanites eschew the train, with the result that the railroads again reduce service, and the inbound traffic lanes become even more clogged.

Question: Will our Connecticut friend change his mind before the New York, New Haven & Hartford expires, and New York's arteries entirely harden?

Answer: Yes, there's hope that he will. Read on.

Nothing said above should be construed to mean that we should all move back to the city from the suburbs, or that we should destroy all our motor cars and walk, or take ship, train or plane for all our journeys. But when we come to such a national pass that our highways are annually strewn with more corpses than any single battlefield, and that our city streets are such fumey, clotted horrors that reasonable men propose closing them to all automobile traffic, then surely something will have to give.

The only way I can see out of our mares' nest is for everyone seriously to ask himself, Why do I live where I live? What must be done about the shape of our towns, suburbs and cities? To what extent must we allow our automobiles to shape our lives for us? What does my car mean to me? Why and when do I really need to drive? What do I really buy when I buy an automobile? Is this what I really either need, or really want?

Anticipating any possible good from such questions presumes a certain degree of confidence in the good sense of the American people, and it further supposes that Detroit is—despite so many indications to the contrary—somehow responsive to the public will. It is my peculiar belief that the public is not always an ass, and that Detroit *is* responsive, after all. The question, Does Detroit, or does the public make taste? is akin to the question, Which came first, the chicken or the egg? Since we are faced, now, with both chicken and egg together, we know the point to be moot, because from now on, ad infinitum, one will breed the other and the other will breed the one. Thus too, with the public and Detroit, as we will shortly see.

At this point, I'd say both the public and Detroit are dead ripe for a little profitable introspection. Some automobile dealers testifying before the Senate nearly three years ago clearly saw what came to pass. They said they feared the overselling in 1955 of overblown dreamboats, marketed as spurious dreams on unsound credit terms, would result in depressed

217

sales years in 1956, '57 and '58. Unfortunately for themselves and for everyone else in the nation, this turned out to be entirely true. Sales not only skidded in '56 and '57, but have proved a fiasco so far into 1958.

Poor sales resulted in factory layoffs and depression in Detroit. Because the nature of our society is so interdependent, and because Detroit's industry is so much at the center of our entire economy, the spectre of a general depression began to haunt the land. Depressions, however, should be regarded as times of hope; as times to learn from mistakes; as times for potentially fruitful examinations of values. It is precisely at such times that more and more men ask themselves what their lives and work really mean. Hence, they may ask themselves, too, what their cars really mean, and our Connecticut commuters may begin to think twice about those trains.

There is no doubt in my mind that Detroit does make definite (although often cynical) gestures toward providing people with that which people are willing to be sold. During the late (and I trust, unlamented) last decade of blind prosperity, Detroit enthusiastically sold what it could sell. Design was not related to the function of the automobile, but was related to the manufacturers' sales and advertising departments. We had all those gadgets; all that trimming. Now, perhaps, is a good time for second thoughts. For instance:

Do you happen to know anyone who really *needs* a temperamental electric motor to crank his windows up and down for him?

Automatic transmissions may occasionally simplify driving problems in stop-and-lurch rush-hour traffic, but they are expensive to begin with, are certainly wasteful of gasoline, are hard on brakes, and are nowhere as safe, responsive and accurate as a pedally operated clutch controlled by a good driver. (And who else should drive?)

A winking red light on the dashboard may forcibly call attention to the fact that you need oil, or that your battery is about to give up the ghost, but then, of course, it may be too late. I take it we all agree that no one should drive a car who is not at least familiar with the basic theory of the machine, and anyone with this rudimentary grasp of things will want to read his instruments to know when the amps in his plant are becoming somewhat scarce, and precisely how scarce. He'll also want to know what the oil pressure is, and not simply to be told that he's running his well dry.

We are entitled to an equally dim view of the "new" air suspension systems in today's cars, inasmuch as *Consumer Reports* tells us that air suspension adds little other than price to the car, and that there are half a dozen automobiles on the market whose standard spring suspensions make for a far more comfortable ride than some of those advertised to be floating on air.

Indeed, some gadgets, like power steering and power braking, can add a quality of danger to those miles of happy motoring. There is that "passing gear" on the automatic transmission, for example. The idea is, if you suddenly jam your accelerator to the floorboards, the engine roars back at you, and after a brief pause you are jerked from, say, 35 miles an hour to 55 miles an hour in a matter of divided seconds. Armed with this contrivance, you can pass the car ahead in much less than normal space and time. The trouble is, a passing gear is a temptation to some weak-minded souls to weave in and out of traffic; to pass when there's just barely room and time to do so. Worse: it sometimes doesn't work, and any time that it doesn't work is obviously the time it's being used, which is the very time it is most urgently needed. Another accessory (that on first glance seems good) is the automatic headlight dimmer that switches to low beam when confronted by the lights of an oncoming car. Trouble is, it also blinks on and off as you ride past bright streetlights, and worse, it doesn't dim your lights when you're following a car.

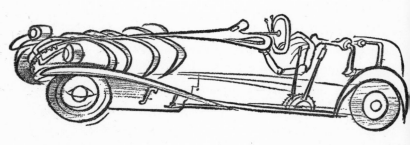

Design by Ettore Bugatti—the real bony non-bulbous thing

One result of such gadgets has been to divorce the driver from practical control and repair of the machine he nominally operates, and we might well wonder whether such a result spells either added convenience or safety. Indeed, the only practical result of many of today's gadgets is to provide a

The Detroit designer

clever salesman with a new assortment of adjectives with which to beguile an unthinking customer.

Likewise, I take it we all agree that three colors and a filigree of chromium adds nothing to the ability of an automobile to do what it is that automobiles are supposed to do, i.e., move from one place to another under their own power. Cars do not swim; why give them fins? Cars do not fly; why somewhat loudly sweep their wings? Cars are not rockets, nor even jets; why claim they are "streamlined"?

Ah, yes, streamlining. If a car were really streamlined, it would resemble a raindrop. There would be no rough surfaces. Everyone knows this. But Detroit claims its models to be streamlined to reduce wind resistance, when this is simply not

221

the case. Not only are today's cars merely one oblong shape perched on a larger oblong shape, but even if the sides and top surfaces are smooth, the undersurface is a nightmare of clutching vacuums and drag-inducing bumps and pits.

Of course, when we discuss styling, we enter the realms of utter fancy. To what purpose are the "simulated" knock-off hubcaps? What dream is served by the solid disc wheels painted to resemble wire spoke wheels? Who is supposed to want the appearance of wire wheels? Who is supposed to be deceived by a strip of chromium into thinking that his automobile is more powerful than it really is? Who actually believes, or cares, or even thinks about Detroit's claim that the metal body is somehow "sculptured"?

Styling, like gadget-addition, boils down to a sales talk, but there must be two parties to a sale. In this sense, the vulgar ostentation of the 1955–58 dreamboat can properly be construed to represent the general vulgar ostentation of the decade 1947–57. True, a great many people even then grumbled about what Detroit was "forcing them to buy," but really there was no force. Such people paid because they liked to imagine they could pay; because their objection to overpriced ostentation was not sufficient to overcome their unthinking acceptance of the idea they should buy a new slather of chromium flatulence instead of, say, buying a secondhand car, fixing up the old car, buying a foreign car, or—in the case of many a man who really didn't need a car—of not buying a car at all. If we look at things in this charitable light, we can't blame Detroit too much for the frightful mess in which it found itself in early 1958. Further, in 1958, the public mood changed from dreamboat-worship to dreamboat-aversion. Now the public mood can, and often does change in a matter of instants, but we've seen that it takes Detroit three years to bring a new design to market. In 1958, poor old Detroit found itself not only oversold, but caught in the middle of a changing dream. There is every reason to think, however, that Detroit has often slowly followed the public mood, and we are currently witnessing one of Detroit's glacial movements in this regard. All major manufacturers intend to produce small cars in 1960. This is the history behind Detroit's decision:

In 1952, when only 27,000 foreign cars were sold in this country, Detroit paid no attention to them. As one dealer said at the time, "there'll always be a few nuts." By 1955, foreign car sales had doubled to 54,000 units. Detroit shrugged: What percentage of 6,000,000 is 54,000?

The following year, 1956, foreign car sales nearly doubled again, to 107,675 units, and Detroit stopped shrugging. The next year, 1957, foreign car sales more than doubled to 225,000, and at that point, Detroit went into conference. In fact, when Detroit brought out its "all new" 1958 models in 1957, it took care to import some of its European cars—automobiles made by Detroit's foreign affiliates and subsidiaries. The idea was, if there's anything to this small car market, small as it was, Detroit wanted in on it. (Typically, General Motors modified its European cars to make them slightly bulkier, heavier be-chromed, and more costly. There are some people who just will never give up that ship.)

E. N. Cole, General Motors' vice president in charge of the Chevrolet division, said in November 1957, that a market of

223

500,000 small car units would certainly "interest" Chevrolet. Ford's R. S. McNamara told the world "that when and if consumer demand for an American small car reaches levels sufficient to justify high-volume production, Ford Motor Company will be ready to supply that demand." At the same time, Ford's J. O. Wright said that Ford could "come close" to turning out a small car comparable in price and quality to the European cars if manufacturing volume was "substantial." Another Fordling, Ernest Breech, defined that volume as 200,000 units. Ironically enough, as each Detroit giant tried to guess the limits of the market, and to figure out what its probable share of that market might be, the elves in the Black Forest who made the Volkswagens had only one regret—they couldn't make Volkswagens for Americans as fast as Americans could order them. In East Coast cities, customers are still cheerfully waiting six to nine months for Volkswagen delivery. Meantime, George Romney's American Motors jumped into the market with its Rambler, and thereby became the only manufacturer to show a sales increase during early 1958.

At this point, may I hoist a small storm signal?

From all I can gather from financial and automobile trade paper accounts, and from conversations with people in the automobile business, Detroit is edging into more or less the right church, but certainly into a wrong pew. Detroit's designers seem to be talking about small cars primarily in terms of size. Detroit's salesmen seem to be trying to divide the population into two classes: those who want big cars, and those who want small cars. Both designers and salesmen seem to be missing the point. The point is, *The virtue of the small European car is not that it is small.*

Consider this for a moment: The fact that a bus is large is no argument against a bus. There is no argument against the size of an El Dorado Brougham if the customer thinks the dimensions of the car exactly match what he imagines to be the El Dorado's function. Thus, if the foreign car's small size is to be considered a virtue at all, it must be so considered only when the purchaser's specific use of the car is such that any larger car would be too big, and any smaller car would be too small.

The real virtues of the European beetles are that they bear something resembling an honest price; that their quality is all the advertising they need; that they are responsive to the driver's control; that they are soundly built and well painted; that their horsepower is no greater than necessary to meet any reasonable demand; that their fuel consumption is low; that their repair rate is equally low; * that their design matches their function; that—in sum—they are a much more adequate means of transportation, dollar for dollar, than any dreamboat Detroit has yet spawned. These foreign cars are unashamedly machines. Just machines. They are not dreams. Their virtues are the virtues of all efficient machines, and these are the virtues I want to see Detroit building into its products. Because I'm an optimist (although certainly a curable one) I think

---

* The operating and maintenance cost of one foreign car is $247 a year below the average cost of operating and maintaining the cheapest of the Big Three's "low priced" models; some other foreign cars cost even less to run and own. The sale price of a foreign car may run $1000 less than the price of one of the Big Three's "low priced" cars.

Detroit may stumble onto the paths of righteousness, if only for the dollar's sake. I am not so foolish, however, as to suppose that an increased, critical public interest in automobiles will be sufficient in itself to do the trick.

Public pressure is valuable, and Detroit obscurely responds to it, but let's not allow this fact to relieve Detroit of any responsibility for original thinking along helpful, rather than mercenary lines. If we are soon to have sensible automobiles, rationally marketed and honestly priced, Detroit will have to think in other than its present terms. For instance, here are a few questions Detroit might profitably ask itself.

Where is the morality in deliberately designing an automobile to meet some defect in a customer's character? No responsible person would give a knife to a man who expressed a desire to stab someone with it. Why then build powerful cars to satisfy the delusions of grandeur of some constitutional psychopaths who wish to relieve their aggressive impulses by whistling through a school zone at 80 miles an hour?

Where is the business morality in selling what you *can*, as compared with the business morality of producing the best machine you can, to sell at the lowest possible price?

What possible excuse is there, other than insensate greed, for dynamic obsolescence? After all, these machines are not summer dresses. They are the most expensive things that most people buy, next to houses. Therefore, what, oh hard-headed Detroit, do you *really* think of selling a man something artificially designed to become obsolete before he's through paying for it? Would you make such a purchase yourself?

Why not, Detroit, make an honest product, honestly priced

226

and honestly advertised? You claim that you cannot publish the real list price your dealers pay for the cars you sell to them, because to do so would be to destroy many a dealer's bargaining position with his customers. Where, do tell us, is the morality in all of this?

Why maintain these lugubrious dealerships, anyway? Perhaps they once had a use, but times have changed, and so have marketing methods. Why not own your retail shops? Why not sell automobiles in supermarkets? If you demand that supermarkets maintain repair facilities and make good on service warranties, automobiles could be sold just as different brands of cans of peas are sold: national prices would be established for each of the various brands. So why not eliminate dealerships—remove those costly middlemen from the customers' backs—supermarket your wares as a thousand other industries do and give us a national list price that has some meaning? As Senator Monroney told you, Detroit, ". . . if honesty in advertising and honesty in pricing were established, the reputation of the product would be enhanced." As you very well know, the reputation of your products could hardly be worse. Or haven't you read last month's sales figure?

At the very least, Detroit, old friend, why not set a precedent and indulge in a spot of honest advertising? Why say a car has 300 horsepower when it actually can't generate 60? Why claim a car has a smooth ride when in fact, on any but a boulevard surface, it rattles the fillings in your teeth and, further, is unsafely suspended?

People drive your products, do they not, Detroit? Then why not return to an automobile that the driver actually drives;

227

And, if you're going to keep on with that lunatic dealer relationship of yours, what are the chances of sending finished cars to dealers, instead of sending along all those things with the unsealed windshields and the loose parts on the back seat floors?

Hey—here's another idea for you to consider, Detroit, old buddy, old pal: How about using a little decent paint? What is it that you use now? Water colors?

Surely there are many questions you can ask yourself, Detroit, and maybe it's high time that you should. Meanwhile, I'm not going to buy another one of your cars until you come up with some good answers.

At this writing, Detroit, the chances of getting any good answers out of you in the near future seem quite remote. While you pay lip-service to the idea of bringing out *some* small cars in 1960, your real feeling was betrayed by your executive who told *The New York Times* this spring that "if the public wants to lower its standard of living by driving a cheap, crowded car, we'll make it."

This smacks evilly of Bourbonism to me. Since when has my standard of living—or anyone else's—ever been measured by the size of my car? Next, assuming that it is, and assuming that you think the standard should be high, what am I to think of you when you show how quickly, how cynically, you are prepared to lower the standard? Surely, the English translation of your man's remark is "We'll do anything for money."

Meanwhile, Detroit, no matter what your attitude toward small cars, it is obvious you see the overblown dreamboat as your main chance. The 1959 models do not indicate that you know we're in the midst of what is charitably called a recession. You frittered away $1,500,000,000 on minor styling changes in this year of vague fear and drift. As *The New York Times* reported, the 1959 cars are "devoid of any radical engineering changes." Instead, they offer "higher style, combined with an even wider and longer silhouette." That billion and a half dollars was spent to put "long, flaired dart-like spears" on Plymouth sterns, the *Times* said, and to slightly lower roofs, add more glass, use anodized aluminum trim, increase the average length of all cars by two inches and that of the Chevrolet by four, and to eliminate the 1958 Chevrolet's rolled-rump effect in favor of fins. Indeed, as the *Times* concluded in its article, you—Detroit—seemed determined to prove in the distressed year of 1958 the truth of the dictum that "whom the gods would destroy, they first make mad."

Instead of being thankful for such gentle, constructive criticism as distinguishes this slim volume, why is it that you seethe, Detroit, whenever anyone suggests that not all your works are sublime? People want what Detroit makes, General Motors keeps saying over and over again, like a petulant child.

"It is not the unemployed people who are causing the recession, but the employed people who refuse to buy at this time," a General Motors vice president told *The New York Times*.

Surely, here is evidence that the gods have already had at you, Detroit. Since when did anyone ever imagine that unemployed people *caused* depressions? And what is a reasonable man to say to the implicit charge that anyone who doesn't buy your products is therefore causing depression, and—in a sense

231

—is thereby committing a most unpatriotic crime?

So far, Detroit, your idea of constructive action has been to suggest, tentatively, that perhaps the companies should advertise national suggested list prices. As long as that irrational dealer relationship endures, however, this can have no meaning at all, for a national list price for a dealership system would have to be put on a basing-point formula like that used to determine phantom freight. In other words, the price would have to be large enough to keep *uneconomical* dealerships in business, with the result that the customers buying from *economical* dealerships would pay over and again more than their car would be worth to anybody. It would seem inevitable that any suggested national list price today would include a factory-installed pack.

Your only other suggestion, Detroit, old comrade, has been the ill-fated and infuriatingly ungrammatical "You Auto Buy Now" campaign, wherein the consumer was told that if he bought a car now twenty-two men would somehow spring back to work. *Consumer Reports* nailed this when it editorially stated the Buy Now campaign was "neither good economics nor good faith.

"It is a trick," *Consumer Reports* continued. "A trick intended to pass on to consumers a heavy inventory of overpriced goods before a deepening of the recession forces price cuts. . . ."

Fortunately enough, the trick didn't work. Despite your furiously thumped tubs, Detroit, sales remained stuck at levels 25 to 30% below 1957's. Even the *Wall Street Journal* thought the whole Buy Now campaign was stupid.

Well, Detroit, old two-tone, it looks as if you'll have to think of something else. Take another tack. Let's hope it will be in the direction of basic morality. Meanwhile, please remember that I am waiting very patiently, and so are at least six million other people.

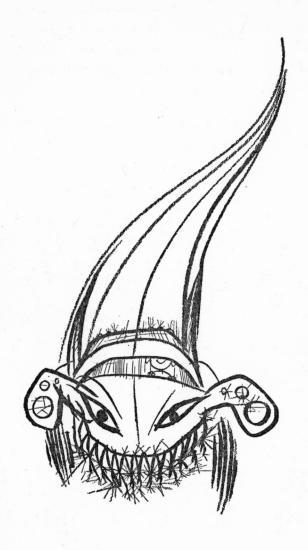